Three Plays :

Produced by
Forest Forge Theatre Company

A Clearing – by Dan Allum
The Gamekeeper – by Josephine Carter
At the Hop – by Shiona Morton

Edited by Sean Aita & David Haworth

Published by Forest Forge September 2008

Forest Forge is supported by the Arts Council England South East; Hampshire County Council; and New Forest District Council.

Printed in the United Kingdom. Cover image by David Bird.

Performance rights: The right to perform these plays is reserved. A license for professional or amateur performance of each of these plays can be obtained, subject to the discretion of the authors, by contacting: Forest Forge Theatre Company, Crow Arch Lane, Ringwood, BH24 SF.

ISBN: 978-0-9559648-0-0

Introduction
by
Nell Leyshon

There is one particular image which I love: the inhabitants of a village take one chair each and carry them through lanes and along paths, and walk to the village hall. Between them they are creating an audience, and with it, a community. The world of rural touring theatre brings that image to life. Every week, throughout the entire country, from the most remote part of Cornwall to the Scottish islands, audiences converge to watch performances of plays, at a shockingly reasonable cost.

Forest Forge is one of the best-loved of the rural touring companies, serving its audience throughout Hampshire and further afield. Each year they send out three full productions, of the best quality. The shows vary, but always include plays written by living writers, especially commissioned by Forest Forge. The plays need to comply with certain criteria: they must have a set which can be transported, along with the cast and crew, in a small van. They must have a maximum of four actors. Preferably some music or singing. Oh, and they also have to please all audiences: from sophisticated theatre goers who may have moved out of London to the New Forest, to people who have only ever seen Forest Forge's work, once per year. The commissioned writers have a real task: to fulfil those criteria, but also to write a play which also pleases them. Sometimes they are asked to write to a brief. Other times they are asked to suggest an idea. The plays cover all themes and subjects, from comedy to the most serious contemporary issue.

Forest Forge has an admirable record in working with writers; sometimes at the beginning of their career, allowing them to cut their teeth and gain a first professional commission;

sometimes when a writer is passionate about a subject which they just know would suit a rural touring audience.

The three plays in this anthology are diverse in theme, but not in quality. They cover a range of subjects, and are written in distinctively different styles. Whether a writer creates a play for the largest London stage, or the smallest village hall, he or she puts in the same amount of work, and it is lovely to think that this publication may lead them on to more future productions, and may cause more people to emerge from their houses and walk along the lanes and paths, to join an audience, build a community, and share an experience.

A Clearing
by
Dan Allum

First Performance: Thursday February 19th 2009

Characters:

Moses Hilldon.
Theodosia Hilldon.
Will Banister.
Clara Banister.

The play is performed in English and Romani.

Act 1 Scene 1

September 1962.

Shave Green Gypsy compound in the New Forest.

Upstage right is the silhouette of an early Gypsy trailer. Beside it is a largish tent with open flaps at the front. Inside the tent we can just about see a made bed on the ground, a small table with food on it, a small wooden barrel, and in the centre there is what appears to be a fire drum, with a chimney that sends smoke out through a break in the roof. A small tree stump is centre stage. Stage left is a kitchen area with sink and breadboard. A set of cupboards is above the washbasin with a window between them. Various cooking utensils are in view. Upstage left is a coat hanger with a workbag at the foot of it, and a table with photos on it. A mirror hangs just to the left of this. Downstage left is a breakfast table and chairs. Upstage centre in silhouette is a bed with a table, chair and a small primus stove beside it.

It is dusk. Snow covers the ground.

On the tree stump sits a young girl. She gently rocks back and forth while mumbling inaudible words to herself. We are unable to see her face, but she is seventeen years old, medium height, slim, and attractive, with long dark hair. The girl is wrapped in many layers of clothing, with a blanket over her shoulders, but is still cold. After a few moments she stops mumbling and slowly lifts her head, glancing around as if fearful someone might be watching. When she is satisfied she is alone the girl begins reciting a poem. Steam rises from her mouth as she speaks into the frosty night air.

THEODOSIA: Amaro ozi hetavavas sar yeck sar o wesh. O bavol si amaro bavol. O pani, amaro rat. O canior amaro tatchipen. Li jin amaro longin yet asarlas chichi, na, ma rokkers kek joller.

Again she glances around before repeating the words.

THEODOSIA: Amaro ozi hetavavas sar yeck sar o wesh. O bavol si amaro bavol. O pani, amaro rat. O canior amaro tatchipen. Li jin amaro longin yet asarlas chichi, na, ma rokkers kek joller.

She drops her head, starts to rock again and resumes the low mumble until the rocking gets faster, more violent and the words more incoherent. A man enters stage right, carrying an armful of firewood. He is in his early forties, tall, roughly handsome and powerfully built. He wears a heavy coat, hat and boots. He watches her.

THEODOSIA: Amaro ozi hetavavas sar yeck sar o wesh. O bavol si amaro bavol. O pani, amaro rat. O canior amaro tatchipen. Li jin amaro..

MOSES: What you sayin, girl?

She stops dead; watches him closely, fearful.

MOSES: Talkin to yourself, again?

Silence.

MOSES: Clear mi path so I can get a fire together. Before we freeze to death.

4

She springs up like a wild animal and clears snow-covered branches from his path. He moves down stage centre and drops the wood in a pile.

MOSES: Findin dry wood in this weather's enough to make you curse God. Where's the paper I give you last night?

She quickly goes to the tent and brings back paper. He uses it as kindling for the fire.

MOSES: I've never known cold like it.

THEODOSIA: Mi feet are numb to mi knees.

MOSES: Feet don't go up that far.

THEODOSIA: Mi legs are froze, then.

He tries to strike a match but it doesn't light.

MOSES: Why ain't you in the tent?

THEODOSIA: It's warmer outside.

MOSES: How you gonna sleep in that blanket tonight, now it's covered in snow?

THEODOSIA: Ain't my blanket, it's yours.

He tries another match that also doesn't light.

MOSES: Matches are drownded. Got any dry?

She takes a box out of her pocket and hands them to him. He strikes one and lights the paper. She wraps her arms around herself for warmth and slowly rocks on her heels.

MOSES: Why don't you move about a bit?

THEODOSIA: I am doin, but it's no good.

MOSES: Then stand still.

THEODOSIA: That's no good either.

He works the fire.

THEODOSIA: Will you rub mi feet?

MOSES: When the fire catches.

She watches the flames.

THEODOSIA: I wiped some of the mud off the trailer while you were gone. I'll wash it properly in the mornin.

MOSES: I thought it was gonna fall to bits on the road. Ain't worth a shillin, and the lorry's tuppence h'apenny. They'll be no calling in that this year. Can hardly pull its self up hill empty, let a lone with a load on.

THEODOSIA: It towed the trailer all the way here with our things on the back.

MOSES: Trailer don't weigh much, and we ain't got a lot. If we can make enough money this winter I'll buy a new motor in the spring.

He puts more wood on the fire.

MOSES: What have you got for tomorrow?

THEODOSIA: There's the linings and lace I sewed on the way down here today. Pegs, shoelaces and lucky charms. We've got some heather left an'all. And I dug some plants out of the snow while you were gettin the wood.

MOSES: Rags and flowers won't put bread on the table, so how are they gonna pay for a new motor?

THEODOSIA: I can do the dukkerin for them that wants their futures told. I could take the pram out, call for rags?

MOSES: They'll be no callin till the weather breaks. You won't get Gadjes out of their kenners in this.

THEODOSIA: How we gonna eat, then?

MOSE: With no coin, it's hotchi witchi.

THEODOSIA: I don't like hedgehog, you know I don't.

MOSES: Bet your life Will's gonner be here tomorrow. There'll be clearin wants doin. The locals'll need diggin out of this. Should be worth a few days pay.

THEODOSIA: What do you want me to do?

MOSES: Take the basket out. Start with them you touched for lovvo last year. You marked their houses?

THEODOSIA: Course.

The fire starts to catch. She squats down to it.

THEODOSIA: That's a chusti bit'a heat, Dad.

MOSES: Fill the kettle and make some tea.

THEODOSIA: Let me warm mi hands first. I can't feel mi fingers.

He puts more wood on the fire and the flames grow higher. He gazes at the tent and blows on his hands.

THEODOSIA: There's scran in the tent if you want it.

He goes to the tent and picks up a thick slice of bread, a lump of cheese and a knife off the table.

MOSES: You hungry?

THEODOSIA: Had mine.

He cuts a piece of cheese, puts it on his bread and eats.

MOSE: You had a chance to dic who's about, yet?

She stands up and gestures across the way.

THEODOSIA: Uncle Jack and Aunt Liza are pulled in their usual place. Next to them bushes over there is Joe boy and Vera. Sam and Charity with their children are next to'em, and Brian and Silvie next to them. Mick and Wip and Bob and Isi are across the way. There's Irish Travellers down the bottom of the lane. And the Buckleys and Prices are through the wesh, with the Lambs and Bartons in the field acai.

MOSES: That all?

THEODOSIA: All I could see.

MOSES: Not as many as last year. We ain't puttin up much of a fight.

THEODOSIA: Uncle Jack said he's sick of fightin. Said the compounds'll be closed in a year or two anyway. No point spillin blood.

MOSES: Too late for that.

THEODOSIA: They ain't gonna fight with us, Dad.

MOSE: Then we'll fight alone.

THEODOSIA: Most of them'll end up in kenners, watch and see.

MOSES: Traveller's have forgot the past and can't see what's comin.

THEODOSIA: Some have got their eye on the army barracks at Broomhills. And the young'uns who got married last year, they've already moved in.

MOSES: Council's backmailing'em and they ain't got sense to see it.

THEODOSIA: Even Jack's got his eye on a house in Totton.

Moses shakes his head, disgusted at the thought.

THEODOSIA: We ain't gonna live in a kenner, are we Dad?

MOSES: They'll have to carry me in feet first.

He crouches down to the fire and cuts more cheese for his bread. He studies Theodosia closely.

MOSES: What was you sayin just now?

She becomes slightly fearful again.

THEODOSIA: When?

MOSES: You know when.

THEODOSIA: I don't.

MOSES: Just now, when I brought the wood here.

THEODOSIA: Nothin.

MOSES: Sounded like somethin.

THEODOSIA: It don't matter.

MOSES: Do to me.

THEODOSIA: I was thinkin to meself, that's all.

MOSES: Nearly can't think loud, you.

THEODOSIA: Dad…

He's getting angry and she becomes more fearful.

10

MOSES: I've told you before.

THEODOSIA: Honest to God!

MOSES: If I catch you again, on my mother's life I'll…

THEODOSIA: I ain't done evil, Dad.

MOSES: You'd better not be lyin to me.

THEODOSIA: I rak sauloholomus I asarlas done narkri. *(I take an oath I haven't done evil)*

He watches her. She stares into the flames. Silence. After a while she tentatively looks across at him and when she thinks it's safe for her to do so she speaks softly.

THEODOSIA: Will you rub mi feet?

He watches her take off her shoe. She puts her foot, which is in a very thick sock, on his lap. He begins to massage her.

Act 1 Scene 2

Next morning.

Lights come up stage left in the Banister house.

Clara stands next to the kitchen sink with her arms folded. She's staring through the window at something outside. She is in her late thirties, quite attractive and dressed in a skirt and blouse with a pinafore wrapped around her waist. After a moment Will enters. He's about forty years old, tall, lean, fit

11

and dressed against the cold. Clara doesn't look at him. She remains concentrated on what's happening outside. He takes off his coat and hangs it up.

CLARA: Snowball fights in September...

She tuts; shakes her head.

CLARA: What kind of mother lets her children out on a morning like this?

WILL: They're just having a mess about before school.

CLARA: There'll be no school today, none tomorrow either. Going to be the coldest winter for two hundred years they reckon.

He begins un-lacing his snow covered boots.

CLARA: You've done a good job clearing the drive.

WILL: Been keeping an eye on me?

Beat

CLARA: Always.

She crosses to the kitchen table and straightens the cloth before sitting down.

CLARA: I didn't hear you get up.

WILL: Tried not to wake you.

CLARA: You're going to work today?

WILL: Afraid so.

CLARA: You'll be the only man in the village who is.

WILL: Got a lane to clear in Minstead.

CLARA: Can't it wait till tomorrow?

WILL: Weather might get worse.

CLARA: Roads will be awful.

WILL: They're not so bad outside the village.

CLARA: You been out already?

WILL: Just to take a look. Car started, which was a bonus.

He crosses to kitchen.

WILL: Anyway, shouldn't you be able to get the gritters out?

CLARA: Not my responsibility.

WILL: One or two words from you will have them quaking in their boots down at the depot.

CLARA: You overestimate my influence. I'm a councillor, not a miracle worker. Though sometimes people do seem to get the two mixed up.

WILL: I thought influence was the name of the game.

CLARA: The name of the game is doing what's best for the community.

WILL: And getting the roads cleared doesn't fall into that category?

CLARA: I'm sure they're on to it, Will. But I'll see what I can do.

He has taken out a loaf of bread, cheese, ham and a jar of mustard from the cupboards and a knife from a drawer.

CLARA: You're not coming back for lunch?

WILL: Might not be able to.

She watches him cut four large slices of bread.

CLARA: You plan on being hungry?

WILL: Thought I'd make one for Moses while I'm at it.

She's surprised at the mention of the name.

CLARA: Is Moses back in Shave Green?

WILL: Saw his trailer enter the compound yesterday afternoon.

CLARA: You never said.

WILL: Didn't think I needed to. It's the time of year.

CLARA: Thought the weather might keep him away.

14

WILL: Hoped you mean.

CLARA: How did he get through the drifts?

WILL: Main roads aren't so bad.

Slight pause.

CLARA: This means we'll have a fight on our hands.

WILL: The majority have all but given in, haven't they? The fight's been bludgeoned out of them.

CLARA: There's still a few left. And Moses is bound to try his best to whip them into a fighting mood. Why can't he just accept the inevitable? Now the Turners and Spencers have moved into housing, and most of the young Travellers are happy to assimilate, you'd think he'd soften up a bit.

WILL: I wouldn't use the words "happy" and "assimilate" when talking about Travellers in earshot of Moses, if I were you.

CLARA: You know what I mean. They're at least trying to get on with the rest of us. And who can blame them? We're offering a clean place to live, with sanitation, electricity and running water.

WILL: It's not home niceties they want.

CLARA: Then what is it?

WILL: Freedom.

She looks across at him.

CLARA: To make other people's lives a misery?

WILL: To live the way they want.

CLARA: While the rest of us pay?

WILL: You'd know more about that than I would.

CLARA: It doesn't matter now anyway, the decision's been made. I was hoping Moses wouldn't be here to kick up a fuss. But so be it.

She watches him making the sandwiches.

CLARA: Why can't he make his own sandwiches?

MOSE: He'll be getting settled in this morning.

CLARA: And preparing food isn't part of settling in?

WILL: It's only a couple of slices of bread.

CLARA: I thought it was his daughter's job to fetch and carry for him?

He stops, throws an annoyed glance her way.

CLARA: *After a moment.* I'm sorry.

He goes back to what he was doing. She rolls a thought over in her mind.

16

CLARA: What do you think his reaction will be to the news?

WILL: You don't need me to tell you that.

CLARA: The man hates the lot of us, always has.

WILL: He's got good reason to hate some.

CLARA: Including me?

WILL: Compounds shouldn't have gone up in the first place.

CLARA: You can't blame today's council for what happened forty odd years ago. It was before most of us were born.

He wraps the sandwiches in a paper bag

WILL: Somebody's got to take responsibility.

CLARA: There was no alternative then. The forest was rife with Gypsies in those days. And it would be again if Moses had his way.

WILL: I don't think it's staying in the forest that matters to him so much. Not really. It's more like he wants us all to remember what was done to his people here. And if there's no Gypsies left, it'll be forgotten.

CLARA: He wants us to feel guilty.

She stares into the distance and speaks half to herself with determination.

CLARA: He'll be wanting for a long time.

WILL: Are they really going to bring in the bulldozers to pull the last few off?

CLARA: Only as a last resort.

He moves across to the coat hanger and puts his sandwiches in his work bag.

WILL: There's something worth remembering that a lot of people forget. Not so long ago he fought for this country. Fought as well as I did, as well as any man did around here.

CLARA: Look, I don't have anything against him personally, you know I don't. But, well, he just causes trouble and spits poison at everyone he meets. And has he ever given you any thanks for the job you got him in the forest?

Putting on his coat.

WILL: You can hardly call what he does for me, a job. He helps us out for a few bob a time when he's needed.

CLARA: The man's about as grateful as a cut snake.

She moves to the sink and begins clearing away.

WILL: Gypsies don't mix. All there is to it.

CLARA: I don't know how they live like it. Or why. Never did.

He begins lacing his boots back on.

CLARA: It's the girl I feel sorry for.

18

She glances across at him.

CLARA: Don't you?

Beat

WILL: Why would I feel sorry for her?

CLARA: You can bet she'll be around again this year with her linings, flowers and charms. And her fortune-telling. As if people haven't got better sense. It's being brought up by a man like that. No wonder she's half insane.

WILL: *Exasperated.* Clara.

CLARA: You've seen the way she goes about the village, talking to herself. We all have.

WILL: She's as right as I am.

CLARA: The girl's touched, Will. Daisy saw her in the forest last year doing some kind of…ritualistic tribal dance in the moonlight.

WILL: For Christ sake!

CLARA: Daisy swears she saw Theodosia Hilldon throwing herself around, as if she was a wild animal, while screaming like a banshee in that God forbidden language they use. Thought she must be putting a spell on someone.

WILL: Probably you.

She stops her clearing.

CLARA: That isn't funny. I'm not the only person on the council you know. I'm not solely responsible for their eviction, though I seem to be the one they're blaming it on. And you know why that is, don't you? Because of you. Because you're always on their side. And because I'm married to you they think I should be too. Well I'm not. I never have been and never will be.

He let's her anger settle.

WILL: Well, the girl would need a pair of snow shoes to dance in this bloody weather, and I don't think Gypsies go in for those. So I think we're safe this winter.

She smiles in spite of herself.

CLARA: Scared poor Daisy to death. Shaking like a leaf she was when she told me.

WILL: Don't take much to put the wind up Daisy, in her condition. Seems like the woman's been pregnant over a year now. When's it finally due?

CLARA: Six weeks. They'll be no work in the office today so I'm going to see her.

She wipes her hands on the cloth, takes off her pinafore and moves to the mirror.

CLARA: I don't mean to slag off the girl. I can't think of anything worse then not having a mother. Apart from perhaps not having a child.

An awkward silence. She watches her refection in the mirror and lightly touches her hair.

CLARA: I'm getting old and showing it. Going greyer by the day. You don't look much different now than you did twenty years ago.

She glances at a photo on the sideboard.

CLARA: No man looked more handsome in a uniform than you. Not even Moses. *She touches the picture.* When the bombs were falling on Southampton I'd think of you far away, and I'd pray so hard my fingers hurt. And when you got back I thought... I had such dreams.

WILL: And I haven't made them come true for you?

CLARA: It's the other way around. Just lately I thought...oh, I don't know. Do you still love me, Will? Do you?

He seems caught off guard.

WILL: I...of course I do.

CLARA: I wish you'd at least tell me once in a while. You used to. I need you to. Sometimes.

She forces a sad smile and goes to where he is standing. She kisses him on the cheek before moving to the window and staring out again.

CLARA: Those poor little mites. I wish their mother would take them in. They're going to freeze to death.

He watches her.

Lights fade out

Act 1 Scene 3

Later that morning.

Gypsy compound.

Moses sits on the barrel downstage centre. He has a knife in his hand and is just finishing off making a batch of pegs for Theodosia to take out and sell. A pile of wood shavings from the work lay at his feet. Will sits on a tree stump stage right. Both men are dressed against the cold.

WILL: We're going to have our hands full clearing the snow from the roads at Hazel Hill and Burley. All but cut off this morning. The woods at Lower Bank will need taking back later on. Then there's ridges and ditches to be cleared all over the forest. There'll be a few weeks work if the snow keeps falling.

MOSES: Anythin for Jack and Sam?

WILL: They here?

MOSES: Pulled in just before we did.

WILL: I didn't recognise the trailers.

MOSES: New since last year. Doin better than we are. But they've got families of children to work for'em.

WILL: We'll give it a couple of weeks to see how it goes. If I can't use them I'll have a word with one or two of the farmers up at Thorney, see if they've got something going. But if what I hear is right, the sprouts and turnips aren't growing, and those that are will likely be frozen to the stems or in the ground.

MOSES: Signs ain't good.

WILL: How was life following the crops this year?

MOSES: Sugar beet and peas weren't bad. Hops in Kent were decent. Weather got the plums and onions before we did.

WILL: Where'd you pull down from this time?

MOSE. Bishops Stortford. Finished the taters last Friday.

WILL: It's a long trek from Hertfordshire in the snow. Was it bad over there?

MOSES: Same as here. But no point waitin for it to clear up cos it ain't goin to.

WILL: You sure about that?

MOSES: Gonna be a bad year.

Moses throws the last pegs into a pile at his feet, folds his knife and puts it in his pocket.

MOSES: I'll put these up for Theodosia. Then I'll be ready.

He picks up all the pegs and puts them in the tent. Will glances around at the encampment.

WILL: Where is she?

MOSES: Gone to fetch water.

WILL: Pulling full churns of water though snow for a mile and a half will keep her fit.

MOSES: Strong as any man in the forest, she is.

WILL: Did she get a chance to learn a little reading this year?

Moses emerges from the tent a little surprised at the question.

MOSES: Why would she wanna do that?

Will takes in the change in Moses' tone.

WILL: She just mentioned she might, that's all.

MOSES: Mentioned it to you?

WILL: No, to a friend of Clara's in the village last year.

Slight pause.

WILL: Nothing wrong in it, Moses.

MOSES: And where would she get the time for that?

WILL: I don't know, evening maybe after she's done a day's work.

MOSES: Ain't said nothin to me.

Beat.

WILL: Moses, I might have to do something at the cabin tonight after we finish work. Are you okay to drop the tools back at my house if I do?

MOSES: If the roads are still clear.

Theodosia appears from behind the wagon. She's struggling with a set of pram wheels that has a wooden box sitting on them. In the box are two milk churns filled with water.

MOSES: *To Theodosia.* You took your time.

THEODOSIA: Roads are like ice. Almost had me in the ditch half a dozen times.

Moses and Will lift the churns from the wheels and put them next to the trailer.

MOSES: Got time for a cup of something hot Will, now the water's here?

WILL: Let's make time.

MOSES: Dosia? *(pronounced Dosha)*

She picks up the kettle and begins pouring water from one of the churns.

MOSE: *To Theodosia.* You sure you didn't take a detour on your way to the water tap?

Picking up on his tone she gives him a quizzical look.

MOSES: Thought you might have dropped into the village.

Will shoots a sharp look at Moses.

MOSES: Will here says you told a friend of his missus up there you wanted to learn to read.

Theodosia looks from Will to her Dad.

WILL: The woman may have got it wrong.

MOSES: *To Theodosia.* Well?

THEODOSIA: I was only saying that bein able to read'd come in handy when we get eviction letters.

MOSES: You don't have to able to read to know what's in them.

THEODOSIA: Gadjes aught to mind their own business.

WILL: I shouldn't have said anything.

MOSES: *To Theodosia with a touch of anger.* Make some tea.

WILL: Maybe we should just get going.

THEODOSIA: *To her father.* He don't want none.

MOSES: We ain't seen him for six months. It's polite.

Moses and Theodosia glare at each other.

26

WILL: I'll have tea if it's no trouble. But if you're going to throw things at each other I'll give it a miss.

Theodosia angrily puts the kettle on the prop that hangs across the fire, spilling some water as she does so. She then goes to the tent and brings three tin teacups.

MOSES: *To Will.* Talkin of eviction, any news about what the locals are plannin on doin with us?

Will puts his hands in his coat pockets. He's been dreading this moment.

WILL: It's not so much the local people.

MOSES: Who then?

WILL: The council.

MOSES: Your wife and her friends talk for the people, don't they?

WILL: Suppose to.

MOSES: Well?

Will glances at Theodosia.

WILL: I'm not sure this is the right time.

Both Moses and Theodosia stare at him.

WILL: It's not good news.

Silence. Moses and Theodosia carry on staring at him.

WILL: This'll be your last year at Shave Green.

Theodosia drops the teacups into the fire. She quickly picks up a stick, kneels down and begins trying to fish them out.

WILL: Be careful!

Will gets up to help her but she pushes him away.

THEODOSIA: I'll do it.

He kneels beside her.

WILL: Let me help.

THEODOSIA: No!

She manages to get all the cups out of the fire. Moses gets up and crosses to fire. Stands over them looking out into the distance.

MOSES: When are they comin?

WILL: Fifth of November.

Beat.

THEODOSIA: Bonfire night.

MOSES: Maybe they want to see some fireworks.

WILL: I don't think so.

MOSES: Maybe they will anyway.

WILL: I hope not, Moses.

Will gets up, moves stage left and brushes dirt from the knees of his trousers.

MOSES: The Lord curse'em all.

WILL: No doubt he already has.

THEODOSIA: No sense cursing Will, Dad.

WILL: I'm not so sure.

MOSES: You're the only man in Shave Green Travellers trust.

WILL: I'm a Gadje.

MOSES: You've been decent to us.

WILL: You've given me no cause not to.

MOSES: We ain't given cause to a lot of people but they still treat us like pigs.

WILL: You're better off out of this place.

Theodosia looks up at Will, shocked.

MOSES: You don't think I know it? The compounds are Gypsy Ghettos. No different from where the Nazis put us before the War.

WILL: Then let the council have the place.

MOSES: They'd like that. Could bury us in the past. Forget we were ever here.

WILL: You'll always be here, one way or another.

Slight pause.

MOSES: I said there'd be ice in Hell before I left this forest.

Will wraps his coat around him to keep in the warmth.

WILL: From the look of this weather, that time might be close.

Act 1 Scene 4

Later that afternoon.

The Bannister house.

We hear voices off before Clara and Moses enter. At first he seems strangely out of place in a house. There is always tension between the two. Clara takes off her coat, scarf, hat and boots but Moses leaves his on as he enters the kitchen.

CLARA: You must be freezing. How you could both go out in this today I'll never know.

MOSES: Work's gotta get done.

CLARA: I know but..

MOSES: Weather could get worse.

CLARA: That's what Will says. You're a couple of pessimists.

He spots the photos on the table. See sees him studying one in particular.

CLARA: Our wedding day.

MOSES: Happy times.

CLARA: They still are, if a little less idealistic.

MOSES: Idealism ain't a bad thing.

CLARA: Depends on the situation doesn't it?

MOSES: Not that I can see.

CLARA: Having unrealistic aims can often lead to getting nothing.

MOSES: Now who's bein a pessimist?

She crosses to him.

CLARA: We all have to make some compromises in life.

MOSES: First I've heard of it.

She smiles, then moves further into the kitchen.

CLARA: I was just on my way back from visiting a friend when I saw you pull up outside. You don't often come this way. But I'm glad I caught you. I thought you'd welcome a minute or two to warm up. I hope you didn't mind me asking you in?

He takes off his hat and puts it on the kitchen table.

CLARA: You've been working in the Minstead area today?

MOSES: Uh huh.

CLARA: Don't know how you managed to get through the snow. Most places are only passable on foot. Would you like a cup of tea, or something stronger?

MOSES: Somethin stronger if it's handy.

CLARA: I think we've got some whisky somewhere.

She begins searching the cupboards.

CLARA: I should thank you for dropping off Will's tools.

MOSES: No need. He's payin me for it.

CLARA: Yes… of course. But thanks anyway. It's not like him to ask you to do it.

MOSES: Said he had somethin to do at the cabin.

CLARA: Did he say what?

Shakes his head, then glances around the place.

CLARA: Will didn't mention anything about it to me this morning. He usually tells me if he's going to be late. Did he say how long he was going to be?

MOSES: No.

She finds the whisky.

CLARA: Ah, here it is.

She tries to unscrew the lid but can't. Reluctantly she hands the bottle to Moses.

CLARA: Do you mind?

He takes the bottle, unscrews the lid with ease and hands it back to her.

CLARA: I won't join you if that's aright. It's a bit early for me and I don't really like spirits.

He watches as she pours the whisky in a glass.

CLARA: By the way, how is Theodosia?

He is surprised by the question.

CLARA: I was talking to my friend about her only today. She must be almost of an age now. I mean girls marry young in your culture, don't they? You must have your hands full fighting the boys off with such an attractive daughter.

MOSES: She'll pair up when it's time.

She turns to face him and holds out the glass.

CLARA: But not yet?

MOSES: What do you want, Clara?

CLARA: I'm sorry?

MOSES: Why'd you asked me in?

CLARA: I told you. I thought you'd welcome a break. It's cold outside.

MOSES: It's been cold before.

CLARA: Not like this.

He stares at her.

CLARA: For God's sake Moses, I'm trying to be polite. Why do you have to be so damned suspicious all the time? Do you want this bloody drink or not?

He slowly takes it and smells the aroma.

CLARA: It's not poisoned.

He takes a small sip, then drinks the rest in one and hands her back the glass.

CLARA: Another?

He picks up his hat from the table and steps in close to her.

MOSES: We ain't movin. I don't care how warm it is in here or how cold it gets outside. We're stayin where we are.

CLARA: Moses, honestly, I only asked you in for...

MOSES: So you're goin to have to bring your friends with their bulldozers and rip us out of the forest cos that's the only way you're getttin rid of us.

She turns away from him and puts the bottle down on the table.

CLARA: I didn't want to discuss that.

MOSES: Then there's nothin else to say.

He turns to leave.

CLARA: All right. The eviction wasn't the reason I asked you in here but now you've brought it up I'll say this. You and your people will never get a better deal then what's on the table now. Each family gets a house of their own. They don't even have to live in it. They can pull their vans in the back gardens and camp there as far as I'm concerned. But they've got to get out of the forest.

He moves back to her.

MOSES: You could offer us ten houses each with gold plated fittins or twenty, and you still wouldn't get us out.

CLARA: I know you will never live in a house Moses, if only to spite everyone who wants you to. So you may have to just pack up your things and move away from here for good. And give us all some peace.

MOSES: What you don't understand is we ain't part of your system. We don't play your games, and we ain't gonna do as we're told like good little children.

CLARA: It's not about doing as you're told. It's about being part of a community.

MOSES: I ain't seen much community sprit shown to Gypsy people lately.

CLARA: I don't see much coming from you, either.

MOSES: Maybe there's a reason for that.

CLARA: I expected there would be.

MOSE: It was your community that marched us into those compounds when it suited them, and now it don't you want to march us right back out again.

CLARA: Your people allowed it to happen. They weren't forced in at gunpoint.

MOSES: And what's the law if it ain't a gun? You make laws that give you what you want then try to force the rest of us to live by'em.

CLARA: This is getting us nowhere. Look, you're a smart man from an intelligent culture. If you learned how to play this so called game you might be able to win it. Don't you understand that? But as long as you scream, shout and refuse to get involved you'll always lose. And why? Because in your language Moses, there's more of us than there are of you. And we're organised.

MOSES: And you're prepared to give up your freedom for a quiet life.

CLARA: We're prepared to compromise if that's what you mean.

MOSES: That's exactly what I mean.

CLARA: Well I call that living.

MOSES: You want to know what I call it?

Beat.

CLARA: No.

Pause. She shakes her head and slowly turns away.

CLARA: No, I don't think I do.

She picks up the bottle.

CLARA: I think I will have that drink after all.

She pours a drink and downs it in one. He goes to the door.

MOSES: If I see your husband on my way home, I'll tell him you're waitin.

He exits.

Blackout

Act 1 Scene 5

Later that night.

Foresters Cabin.

Dim lights come up stage centre on the bed, table, chair and small primus stove that warms the room. Will sits in the chair, and has his elbows on his knees. He looks as if he's been waiting for a while. After a moment he gets up, walks to the window and looks out into the darkness. He pulls out a packet of cigarettes from his coat pocket, takes one out, lights it, takes a drag and blows smoke across the room.

Silence.

There is a knock at the door. He moves across the room and pauses before opening it. Theodosia is standing there. She is heavily dressed against the cold. She doesn't look at him. He motions her to come in and she enters with her head down as if embarrassed to be there. She walks directly over to the primus stove and sits on the floor next to it. After warming her hands she takes out a packet of tobacco from her pocket, some cigarette papers and is about to role her own when Will offers her one of his. She shakes her head and carries on rolling her own. When her cigarette is rolled she lights it with her own matches.

WILL: How are your fingers, Dosia?

She instinctively lifts her hand to her month and gently licks the tips of her fingers.

WILL: Thought you were going up in flames this morning.

THEODOSIA: Part of me did.

WILL: Compound had to close sooner or later.

THEODOSIA: You said you were glad.

WILL: No.

THEODOSIA: Said we'd be better off "out of this place".

WILL: It's not the same thing.

THEODOSIA: Is to me.

WILL: Forty years is long enough.

THEODOSIA: That ain't what I meant.

WILL: I know what you meant.

Pause.

THEODOSIA: Did you want me to come here tonight?

WILL: You know I did.

She looks at him for the first time.

THEODOSIA: How would I know after what you said this mornin?

WILL: What I said had nothing to do with you. With us.

Beat.

THEODOSIA: Are they really gonna pull us out of the forest?

WILL: Unless you move first.

THEODOSIA: Bostaris! *(Bastards)*

She gets up and moves across the room. After she becomes calmer she looks around the place.

THEODOSIA: I must have dreamed about bein back here every night since I left. Six months felt like ten years this time. And now we've only got a few weeks. Is it your wife's doin?

WILL: Partly.

He moves to the chair and sits down.

WILL: She's suspicious.

THEODOSIA: Of me?

WILL: Of me. I haven't been able to stop thinking about you since you left. It's getting in the way of things.

THEODOSIA: Gettin in the way? I ain't hardly been able to sleep since I seen you last. I'm skin and bone through not eatin. Just look at the state of me.

She takes off her coat and lets it fall to the floor. He watches her body for a long moment. They make strong, sexual eye contact.

THEODOSIA: The days go on forever, and the nights...

She looks away.

THEODOSIA: They're burnin me up.

WILL: We have to be careful. Someone from the village saw you dancing near here before you moved last year.

She looks at him in fear.

WILL: It's okay. No one you know.

THEODOSIA: Mush or manushi?

WILL: A woman. She thought you were putting a spell on someone.

THEODOSIA: They think I'm a chohawni, now?

WILL: You could be a witch for all they know. Villagers around here don't get out much.

Beat.

THEODOSIA: The dance...it was after I left here.

WILL: I know.

THEODOSIA: The night before we moved. I was sayin goodbye to the forest...and to you.

She faces away from him.

THEODOSIA: I've gone over that night a thousand times in me head.

WILL: Perhaps I shouldn't have said those things.

She's horrified.

THEODOSIA: You're sorry now?

WILL: Not sorry but...

THEODOSIA: Please don't take'em away from me.

WILL: I'm not taking anything away.

THEODOSIA: You said you...cared about me, that I was beautiful. You said...

WILL: I meant every word.

Beat.

THEODOSIA: I always had feelins for you, Will. Even when I was young and you used to come to our wagon and talk to me dad. I'd watch you from behind the curtains. I... felt things.

WILL: Whenever you're close to me, I don't know who or what I am anymore.

She takes off her soft hat revealing a headscarf underneath.

THEODOSIA: Dad caught me sayin one of mum's poems last night.

WILL: *Concerned.* You get his belt?

She shakes her head.

WILL: You said it in front of him?

THEODOSIA: I didn't know he was there.

She looks across at him.

THEODOSIA: Amaro ozi hetavavas sar yeck sar o wesh.

WILL: Our hearts beat as one with the forest.

THEODOSIA: O bavol si amaro bavol.

WILL: The wind is our breath.

THEODOSIA: O pani, amaro rat.

WILL: The streams, our blood.

THEODOSIA: O canior amaro tatchipen.

WILL: The silence, our truth.

THEODOSIA: Li jin amaro longin yet asarlas chichi, na, ma rokkers kek joller.

WILL: It knows our longing, yet regrets nothing, nor whispers no goodbyes.

A pause.

THEODOSIA: I'm tired of having to speak her words in secret. He don't care about me anyway. He only cares about her. I'm sick of comin second. He still thinks I'm a child, but I'm desh ta eft. A woman!

WILL: In your culture.

Beat.

THEODOSIA: Then make me a woman, in yours.

Lights begin a slow fade as he moves close up behind her.

THEODOSIA: Last night, in mi bed, when I was only half awake, a vision come to me. There was this stack of hay bales, in an open field. Dry in the heat they were, under a bakin hot sun. I kept tryin to set light to'em with matches. I'd strike one, hold it close, and when the bale started to burn I'd spit on the flames. Mi saliva was enough to douse'em. When the danger passed I'd light another one. I kept on like that till mi spit ran out, and the whole stack was ablaze. Then, when it was burnin at its most fierce, a snake appeared at its centre then dragged itself towards me. I was frightened and shut mi eyes. But as it wound its self around me I could feel mi blood gettin hot. And when its tongue licked mi body like flames, sweat flowed from me like a waterfall. When the snake reached mi face it sank its fangs into mi lips, and poison gushed into mi mouth. Oh… Will, the feelins I had. *Almost overwhelmed.* And the shame.

She looks at the floor in shame before lifting her head again.

THEODOSIA: When I opened my eyes the snake in the fire… it was you.

44

He reaches out and takes off her headscarf and lets it fall to the floor.

WILL: Tute are miro odjus Romani rakli. (*You are my beautiful Romany Girl)*

THEODOSIA: Tute are miro rinkeno weshengro. (*You are my handsome man of the forest.)*

With her body shaking and hardly able to breathe she kisses him with tremendous tenderness. He undresses her as she winds herself around him. Slowly the kisses turn to deep animal passion. As they lose themselves in rapture, a silhouetted figure appears at the window. And as the lights fade further, with the lovers in shadow, we can clearly make out the figure of Clara, watching them.

Blackout

Act 2 Scene 1

Six weeks later. 4th November. Late afternoon.

Gypsy compound.

Spotlight comes up on Theodosia who is sitting down stage centre with various flowers, moss and heather around her. At present she is dividing individual heather strands into sprigs to sell. At first she is engrossed in what she is doing, but then gets lost in a memory.

THEODOSIA: Beautiful the woodland, stillness in motion, babblin conversation goes rollin, trippin and dancin by. I am lost in a daydream, with the fragrance of whispered meanins, and a memory of the one, adored.

Lights slowly fade up as Theodosia carries on binding heather. The flaps to the tent are closed and several dead rabbits and pheasants hang by the fireplace outside. Theodosia has been skinning rabbits for supper and still has specks of blood on her hands. A washing line is tied between the trailer and a tree with several garments of clothing hanging on it. A tin bath of water sits close by which has been used for washing the clothes. The barrel is far stage right.

Clara enters upstage left and watches Theodosia before she is seen. She takes a few steps forward and when Theodosia becomes aware of her presence she turns to face her. Theodosia gets up as Clara approaches.

Silence.

THEODOSIA: Mi father's still workin.

CLARA: It's not your father I've come to see.

Theodosia watches closely as Clara moves downstage centre looking around the place.

THEODOSIA: You want to buy somethin?

CLARA: Perhaps.

THEODOSIA: I've got flowers, heather, pegs, shoelaces, charms and the like.

Clara looks at the goods at her feet.

CLARA: I'll take a bunch of lucky heather.

Theodosia picks up a sprig of heather.

THEODOSIA: That'll be a penny.

Clara gives her money and Theodosia hands her the heather. Theodosia then kneels down and begins filling the basket with her goods. Clara moves stage right.

CLARA: It's been a long time since I was in this part of the forest. I used to come here when I was a child. My parents didn't live far away. They were a little wary of Gypsies in those days, and warned me against playing with them in the wood. But I'd still come.

A slight pause.

CLARA: Where will you move to, tomorrow?

THEODOSIA: We ain't goin nowhere

CLARA: I see.

THEODOSIA: Mi father'll be back soon wantin food and I've got to get the shooshi's skinned and boiled.

CLARA: The what?

THEODOSIA: *Gesturing to the dead rabbits.* Them.

CLARA: Oh, rabbits. I...

Clara looks at the specs of blood on Theodosia's hands.

CLARA: Looks like a job that's already been done.

Theodosia stares down at her own hands.

CLARA: I won't keep you long.

Clara sits on the barrel.

CLARA: I used to see you a lot around the village selling your wares. In my street too. But I haven't seen you this year.

THEODOSIA: I've been about.

CLARA: To my street?

THEODOSIA: Must have.

CLARA: Recently?

THEODOSIA: Suppose so.

CLARA: When?

THEODOSIA: Last week maybe.

CLARA: You came to my door?

THEODOSIA: Probably.

CLARA: I was home most of last week. I didn't see you.

THEODOSIA: Perhaps you was round the back and didn't hear me knockin.

CLARA: What day was it?

THEODOSIA: Can't rightly remember.

CLARA: Daytime or evening?

THEODOSIA: Couldn't rightly say. What difference do it make?

CLARA: I was just wondering why I hadn't seen you, that's all.

Theodosia takes the basket of goods and puts it in the tent.

CLARA: Do you still tell fortunes?

THEODOSIA: *Emerging from the tent behind Clara.* I do, yeah.

CLARA: Think you could tell mine?

THEODOSIA: I reckon I could.

CLARA: I'm not sure I believe in that kind of thing.

THEODOSIA: Don't have to.

CLARA: No?

THEODOSIA: Just trust.

CLARA: Trust you?

THEODOSIA: No. You. You'll know if I ain't tellin the truth.

CLARA: How much does it cost?

THEODOSIA: Half a crown.

CLARA: That's a lot of money.

THEODOSIA: To know what tomorrow's gonna bring?

Pause. Clara takes out her purse, searches it and brings out some coins.

CLARA: Two shillings.

THEODOSIA: Ain't enough.

CLARA: I haven't got anymore.

THEODOSIA: You sure?

CLARA: It's all there is.

Theodosia takes the coins, walks back to the tent, opens the flap and waits for her.

CLARA: We have to go in there?

THEODOSIA: Uh huh.

CLARA: Can't we do it out here?

THEODOSIA: You frightened of the dark?

Slowly Clara enters the tent and Theodosia follows. Inside, a cloth covers the ground. There is a bedspread out at the back, a small box in the corner with two chairs beside it and an up turned box to the side. The fire is lit in the stove, centre.

CLARA: You sleep in here?

THEODOSIA: Mi father. I sleep in the trailer.

Lights fade slowly during the early part of the scene leaving only a red glow in the tent from the firelight. Theodosia arranges the two chairs so they are facing each other. They sit. Theodosia tentatively reaches out her hand for Clara's.

CLARA: I want to know something about you first.

THEODOSIA: About me?

CLARA: If you don't mind.

THEODOSIA: What difference do it make who I am?

CLARA: It would feel more...real. Personal.

THEODOSIA: It ain't supposed to be personal.

CLARA: You're going to tell me about my personal life, aren't you?

THEODOSIA: It don't work like that.

CLARA: Just tell me, a little. Anything.

Theodosia shakes her head.

CLARA: I can't do it otherwise. I'll have to ask for my money back.

THEODOSIA: *After weighing up the situation.* I'm a Traveller. There's nothin more to tell.

CLARA: How old are you?

THEODOSIA: Seventeen.

CLARA: Have you always travelled around?

She nods.

CLARA: You've never lived in a house?

Shakes her head.

CLARA: You've been to school?

THEODOSIA: No.

CLARA: But you can read?

Shakes her head.

CLARA: You like the work you do?

She shrugs.

CLARA: You could get a factory job, so could your father.

THEODOSIA: He'd rather shovel shit then take orders from another man.

CLARA: He takes them from Will.

THEODOSIA: Will ain't like...

CLARA: Other men?

Beat.

CLARA: When you move from here, whenever that is, where will you go?

THEODOSIA: Depends.

CLARA: What will you do?

THEODOSIA: This and that. Why do you live in one place?

CLARA: Stability I suppose, a sense of belonging.

THEODOSIA: People belong to the earth, to the trees, the wind and rivers. Nothin else.

CLARA: What about God?

THEODOSIA: Bible stories are for keepin children quiet.

CLARA: Sounds like something your father would say.

THEODOSIA: How do you know what mi father would say?

CLARA: He brought you up alone, didn't he?

THEODOSIA: *With a trace of anger.* Do you want your fortune told or not?

CLARA: I remember her you know, your mother.

Theodosia's anger is now laced with interest.

CLARA: We were both about the same age. I first saw her around the village when I started school. She was selling trinkets even then. And we worked together in the forest during the war, picking black watch. They'd take it to the factories to make gunpowder. We cleared the place of it while our men were gone.

THEODOSIA: What do you want?

CLARA: Do you know after the Germans had done their damnedest over Southampton, their bombers would sometimes drop whatever load they had left around here to lighten their planes, before flying home?

THEODOSIA: We never had no air raid shelters. Had to hide under the wagons.

CLARA: Then the awful sound of the doodle-bugs going over. You could hear the sirens from here as clear as day. There must be lots of unexploded bombs in the forest.

THEODOSIA: Children still find'em here sometimes. We tell the gavvers...

Realising Clara doesn't understand the word.

THEODOSIA: The police.

CLARA: I suppose your father tells you all about those times.

THEODOSIA: He ain't one for talkin about the past.

CLARA: Not ever?

THEODOSIA: Nothin.

CLARA: Why do you think that is?

THEODOSIA: He'll be back in a minute, you can asked'im.

Clara senses time is running out.

CLARA: I also remember the night you were born. And the days and nights that followed. I helped her, your mother. Your grandmother delivered you, she must have said? I did as much as I could for Amberline but the infection was too deep.

The sound of her mother's name almost takes Theodosia's breath away. Clara starts to slightly lose her composure and a pleading tone enters her voice.

CLARA: I tried to keep the fever down. I was the one who brought the doctor. Even though it was too late by then, I brought him. You know that, don't you?

Theodosia stares at Clara half in anger and half in disbelief.

CLARA: And then the burning of her…wagon. It shocked the community, even in wartime.

THEODOSIA: You'd better go.

CLARA: I need you to listen to me.

THEODOSIA: I don't want you here no more.

CLARA: You owe me for what I did, Theodosia. You owe me… something.

THEODOSIA: I owe you?

Theodosia gets up and goes to the tent opening.

THEODOSIA: Get out!

CLARA: You're the image of her, you know.

THEODOSIA: Get out!

Clara gets up and goes to her.

CLARA: Some things are worth dying for. A child is worth dying for. Your father doesn't know how lucky he is to have felt a child's hand reach out to him. To have felt its breath on his face and know it was he who helped give her life. I've never known that. I never will. I'll only ever be half alive. There's only one thing that keeps me breathing.

Theodosia is finally hit by the realisation of why Clara is there.

THEODOSIA: Your marriage.

CLARA: There's nothing more important in my life than Will. And there's nothing more important to Will than me, though sometimes he doesn't realise it. I'd hate for him to wake up one morning and find he's lost the one thing he genuinely loves. We may not have the excitement or passion any more, but deep down we have the love. It's enough for me; but for Will...

Clara, close to tears reaches out her hand to Theodosia and opens her palm.

CLARA: Is my marriage going to last till I die? I'm afraid that after tomorrow, or whenever it is you leave, something of Will is going with you. Something I'll never get back. *Lifting her palm closer to Theodosia's face.* Can you tell me if I will have my marriage, Theodosia? Please... can you... please, tell me that?

Theodosia is about to speak when voices are heard outside. Lights come up as both women move outside the tent. Moses and Will enter stage right. They all see each other.

A shocked silence.

WILL: Clara...

Beat

MOSES: Dosia?

Silence

CLARA: Hello, Moses.

MOSES: *To Clara.* Didn't think the fireworks started till tomorrow.

CLARA: I'm not here as a councillor.

MOSES: *Noticing the sprig of heather in her hand.* You come lookin for luck?

CLARA: *To Will.* I didn't think you'd be back, yet.

THEODOSIA: *To Clara.* I told you.

WILL: Job in Christchurch didn't take as long as I thought. Clara, what are you doing here?

MOSES: I would've thought that was plain.

CLARA: *To Moses.* I'm not here to gloat.

MOSES: You ain't here to buy flowers, either.

CLARA: *To Moses.* If I had known you'd be here I wouldn't have come.

WILL: I think you'd better leave.

MOSES: *To Theodosia.* What's she after?

WILL: Now listen Moses.

MOSES: *To Theodosia; gesturing to tent and ignoring Will.* What were you two doin in there?

THEODOSIA: I was tellin her fortune.

WILL: Telling her what?

CLARA: My fortune.

MOSES: So what's life gonna bring you?

She glances at Theodosia.

CLARA: I'd better be going.

MOSES: You'd better be stayin. Least till I find out what's going on.

THEODOSIA: Nothin's going on.

MOSES: Hoffeno!

WILL: She's telling the truth, Moses.

MOSES: How would you know?

Small explosions can be heard in the background from far away fireworks.

MOSES: Seems like some people can't wait till Guy Fawkes. You should know better than to take her in our home.

THEODOSIA: She paid two shillins.

MOSES: Judas silver.

WILL: Take it easy.

MOSES: Give it back to her.

THEODOSIA: Dad...

CLARA: I don't want it.

MOSES: Give it back or I'll take your face off.

Theodosia takes the money out of her pocket and offers it to Clara.

CLARA: I don't want it.

MOSES: Take it.

THEODOSIA: You'd better take it.

Clara shakes her head. Moses takes a step toward Clara but Will moves to block him.

MOSES: Stand out the way, Will.

Will doesn't move.

MOSES: *Squaring up to him.* I ain't askin you again.

WILL: I don't expect you to.

The men face each other in silence for a long, dangerous moment.

MOSES: Then you'd better take your shirt off.

WILL: I don't want this.

MOSES: Then step aside.

Will still doesn't move so Moses takes a couple of steps back and takes off his coat and begins unbuttoning his shirt. After a moment Will does the same.

CLARA: Are you both, mad?

They both ignore her.

CLARA: Are you actually going to fight each other like animals?

Clara turns to Theodosia who is watching the men with fascination.

CLARA: Are you just going to just stand there?

THEODOSIA: Let'em fight.

CLARA: For God's sake!

Both men are stripped to the waist, facing each other. It's clear from the way they frame up both men have boxed before, probably in the Army. They begin to circle each other. Clara runs between them.

MOSES: Get her out of the way, Will.

WILL: Clara, get back.

CLARA: No.

MOSES: Get her out of here.

WILL: Don't touch her, Theodosia.

THEODOSIA: Stand back, Clara.

MOSES: Dosia!

THEODOSIA: Get out of the way woman, you'll get yourself hurt!

CLARA: Is this about money? Whether or not I take it back? Here, I'll take it. I'll take it.

She goes to Theodosia and takes the money from her hand and throws it into the trees.

CLARA: There, it's gone. Now will you please stop this!

MOSES: It's too late for that.

CLARA: You mean you're still going to fight?

WILL: Go home, Clara!

Moses throws a left jab, which falls a couple of inches short of Will's jaw. Will tries to counter with a left hook that misses Moses' head by a whisker.

CLARA: You are both insane!

Moses fades to the right, steps forward on his left foot and throws a left hook to Will's ribs that makes Will wince in pain. Moses then throws a right cross at Will's head but Will sees it coming and ducks back just in time and throws a right hook of his own which lands on Moses' cheek, knocking him back a couple of paces. Both men take a moment, frame up and begin to circle again. Clara screams.

CLARA: All right! I'll tell you why I came here.

All ignore her.

CLARA: I came here to tell you it's okay to stay Moses. The council will let you stay!

Theodosia looks at Clara in shock. Both men stop what they are doing for a moment and look at Clara.

CLARA: Isn't that true, Theodosia?

Theodosia looks blank.

CLARA: I asked the council this morning to let you stay till after Christmas. I'm not sure what they're going to do. I can't guarantee anything but they're thinking it over. Isn't that true, Theodosia?

All look at Theodosia. Silence.

CLARA: Theodosia, for God's sake isn't that true?

Pause

THEODOSIA: Yeah. That's what she said.

Theodosia spits on the ground.

MOSES: Why would you do that?

CLARA: Why? Why? Well... because... of the weather. It would be cruel to throw anyone out of the forest in this.

MOSES: Why didn't you say that in the first place?

CLARA: I would have done, if you hadn't been so pig headed.

Moses looks at Will and after a moment drops his arms. Will does the same.

MOSES: What time will you know?

CLARA: First thing in the morning. No later than the afternoon. I'll let Will know and he can tell you.

Moses slowly goes to his shirt, picks it up and puts it on before grabbing his coat.

MOSES: I'm going for firewood. I'll talk to you, later.

He exits.

A long silent, ominous moment is shared between the three of them. Each knows a decision has to be made here, now.

CLARA: Will, are you coming home with me?

He looks at Theodosia. She has a beseeching look and gently shakes her head for him not to go.

WILL: Yes.

As Theodosia watches him, tears of pain and rage fill her eyes. She picks up Will's shirt and coat, moves closer and throws them at him. After a moment he picks them up, then he and Clara exit. After watching them go Theodosia sees the sprig of heather that Clara has dropped on the ground. She picks it up, studies it for a long moment then slowly lets out an animal cry of pain.

Act 2 Scene 2

Later that evening.

The Bannister house.

Clara sits at the kitchen table with her head in her hands. Will has his back to her as if looking out of the window.

WILL: Fortune telling?

CLARA: One thing led to another.

WILL: You going to meet a tall dark handsome stranger?

CLARA: Would you care if I did?

WILL: You lied about getting the eviction stopped.

CLARA: I didn't know what else to say. You both seemed intent on killing each other so I said the first thing I thought might save lives.

WILL: What are you going to do now?

CLARA: The evictors aren't due at the camp till tomorrow afternoon. I'll go to the office first thing in the morning and tell them.

WILL: Tell them what exactly?

CLARA: Well... I don't know yet. That... Theodosia slipped and hurt herself, or Moses got food poisoning from one of the rabbits or pheasants he's poached, or they've all got rabies up there and the whole place is highly contagious. I don't know. But I'll think of something.

WILL: And if you can't?

CLARA: I'll do it!

He turns to face her.

WILL: What on earth got into you? Did you expect them to welcome you with open arms?

CLARA: I didn't think you'd both come crashing in like that. I thought it was going to be just me, and Dosia. And I had to do something. The girl...thinks she's in love with you.

As if incredulous, he tries to brush it off.

WILL: That's ridiculous.

CLARA: I don't think so. And you know better than that.

WILL: Well, a crush maybe.

CLARA: It's not really her feelings for you I'm worried about.

WILL: Then what?

She tries to speak but can't get the words out.

WILL: They'd have been gone tomorrow anyhow, or soon after.

CLARA: Yes but I thought… I thought part of you might have gone with them.

WILL: Oh, come on Clara.

She is trying to hold herself together.

CLARA: I didn't know what else to do.

WILL: You should have talked to me about it.

CLARA: Talked? How could I talk to you? When…

WILL: When what?

CLARA: When…when I…

He stares at her as if uncomprehending.

CLARA: *Stealing herself with every ounce of her being.* I saw you… together.

Pause.

WILL: You saw..,

CLARA: In the cabin.

Slight pause.

WILL: No, Clara.

CLARA: Will.

WILL: You couldn't have. She's never…

CLARA: Please!

WILL: I want to know. When do you think…

CLARA: Don't ask me any questions.

WILL: But you have to tell me when you…

CLARA: I said please don't ask me anything! For God's sake Will, don't! Just don't!
She breaks down. He makes a move toward her but stops himself. After she recovers herself she speaks.

CLARA: I saw you… together... no use trying to deny it now, or… hide it… anymore.

He watches her, helpless and lost.

CLARA: These last weeks have been…

She almost breaks down again but swallows her pain this time.

CLARA. There's just two things I want to know. Do you love her? Do you want to be with her?

A long silence.

WILL: She's; just a child.

CLARA: Yes, that's exactly what she is. A beautiful, exciting and confused child.

WILL: Confused?

CLARA: Yes of course confused. Wouldn't you be if you'd been brought up by a man like, Moses? The girl can't mention her dead mother's name in his presence without getting her face slapped. The love she craves from her father isn't there so she turns to the next best thing.

He moves to the chair stage left. She stares after him.

CLARA: We've been married a long time. What we've got isn't perfect but it's precious to me. And it's something I don't want to lose.

WILL: We're not going to lose anything.

She studies him hard.

CLARA: Will; has the reason you went with her got anything to do with me? I mean, am I doing something wrong?

WILL: No.

He is unable to look at her.

CLARA: Do I mean anything to you anymore?

WILL: Of course you do.

CLARA: Then for Christ's sake tell me, because I'm not a bloody mind reader!

WILL: I want you, Clara. I want us.

CLARA: Do you? Do you really?

WILL: Yes.

CLARA: And I want you. So much.

She watches him with a mixture of love, pain and resignation.

CLARA: Are we… together?

WILL: If you still want us to be.

A long pause. She tries to smile through her tears.

CLARA: How are your ribs?

WILL: My ribs? A couple are cracked, I think.

She gets up and moves across to him.

CLARA: Let me take a look.

He stands up, lifts his shirt and shows her where he was hit by Moses. She touches him. He winces.

CLARA: You could be right.

She moves closer to him and begins tucking in his shirt.

CLARA: Daisy had her baby this morning. In all the excitement I forgot to tell you. A boy. Guess who volunteered to be chief baby sitter? I want to tell you something. You don't have to say anything, just listen. Okay? Nothing will ever take the place of the child we'll never have. Don't you think that's sad, or funny even? I do. Sometimes I laugh about it, but mostly I cry. Did you know that? I cry. When I'm on my own of course. Not when I'm with people, especially not when I'm with you because you don't like to see tears. You don't want to look at pain. Makes you feel guilty because you don't believe you can do anything to ease it. Well you can. You ease my pain just by being here, with me.

She moves upstage right to the entrance.

CLARA: You can see her one more time Will, to say goodbye and wish her well. You're not the answer to her problems. I'll see you in a little while.

She exits.

Fade to blackout.

Act 2 Scene 3

Later that night.

Gypsy compound.

It is snowing. Moses and Theodosia sit in the tent by the fire. Moses has a bruise on his left cheek from Will's punch. An ominous silence hangs in the atmosphere. Theodosia glances across at her father now and again as if daring herself to say something. Finally she speaks.

THEODOSIA: What was she like?

MOSES: Who?

THEODOSIA: Mi mother?

He shifts uncomfortably.

MOSES: Your grandmother's got a mouth bigger than ten people. I'm sure she's told you everythin you want to know about her.

THEODOSIA: I want to hear it from you.

He speaks without turning to her.

MOSES: Get the rest of the things packed for the mornin. Whether they're coming or not we want to be ready for'em.

THEODOSIA: Everythin's packed. We'll be ready.

Beat.

THEODOSIA: What was she like?

MOSES: It ain't time for this.

THEODOSIA: Then when will it be time?

MOSES: It's better left.

THEODOSIA: I want to know.

MOSES: Why now?

THEODOSIA: I'm old enough.

MOSES: I said why now, tonight, in this place?

He watches her for a long moment and slowly it dawns on him.

MOSES: Clara. *Smiles, half triumphantly.* I knew it weren't right what she said. What did she really come for today?

THEODOSIA: I told you, the eviction.

MOSES: Oduvvos hokkano!

THEODOSIA: I can't tell you, Dad.

MOSES: Theodosia.

THEODOSIA: I feel sick.

MOSES: You'll feel better when you've told me. What did she say to you?

Theodosia gets up and steps out of the tent and into the snow. She looks dazed, unsteady on her feet, swaying slightly from side to side. He watches her from the tent as she retches then recovers.

THEODOSIA: She talked about wartime, about working in the forest, about when I was born… and about mi mother dyin.

Deep anger explodes in him now. He stares across at her and with clenched fists speaks in whispered rage.

MOSES: She had no business…

THEODOSIA: I'm glad she did. I'm glad somebody did. Mi mother's like a weshimulo who nobody mentions cos they're scared of what's gonna happen to'em. They're frightened of you, Dad.

MOSES: You've said enough.

THEODOSIA: She deserves more.

MOSES: I said enough!

She's caught in two minds about what to do. She makes her choice and turns to face him.

THEODOSIA: In all these years I've never heard you once call her by name.

MOSES: *Menacingly.* Theodosia.

THEODOSIA: I'm tired of it. I'm fed up with runnin, hidin, talkin in secret and bein frightened of you.

MOSES: You've had your warnin.

THEODOSIA: I ain't got anythin of hers, Dad. No photos, no memories, no nothin. All I've got are her poems, and if Granny hadn't taught'em to me I wouldn't have them.

His body trembles with the effort of holding back his anger.

THEODOSIA: Why don't you say it Dad? Say her name.

He slowly gets up and moves towards her. She takes a couple of steps back.

THEODOSIA: You think it was my fault she died don't you? If I hadn't been born she wouldn't have died. If that's what you believe then say it. Say her name Dad, and say her dyin was my fault.

She stops backing away and instead steps forward.

MOSES: What's that woman done today? What's she put between us?

THEODOSIA: What's between us is a dead woman. And Clara didn't put her there. You did.

He slaps her across the face and she falls to the ground. She gets up to her knees, retching as she does so. Finally she gets to her feet and crosses back to him. A trickle of blood runs from her mouth. She defiantly stands in front of him.

THEODOSIA: I can't live like this anymore. It's dark…so much pain. I can't… pretend any more.

MOSES: Nobody's pretendin, nothin.

THEODOSIA: She died here, in this forest. We'll be gone soon. Tell me about her…please!

MOSES: What good would it do? We've just got to get on with our lives.

THEODOSIA: What lives? You're as dead as she is…and I may as well be.

Starting to weep she falls to her knees and holds out her arms to him.

THEODOSIA: Help me…Dad…help me!

She lowers her hands and starts to dig in the snow with her fingers. In her fear, pain and cold she seems close to delirium.

MOSES: What are you lookin for? Dosia, what are you lookin…

THEODOSIA: We've got to find her. She's under here I know. We've got to find her… then she can rest… and we can live.

He watches her in the snow, finally appalled at her pain.

MOSES: Dosia… child…

He goes down on his knees to her, puts his arms around her and pulls her to him.

MOSES: She ain't under there. She's here…she's here. I'll tell you about her. I'll tell you.

He too begins to cry. He rocks her like a baby in his arms.

76

MOSES: *Talking fast, desperate to reassure her.* Wild she was but soft. Amberline, your mother. Easy hurt. She felt things different to most people. It's how come she could make up her stories. Poems. No other Traveller I know could do it.

THEODOSIA: You brought me up.

MOSES: Dragged you up more like. I've been too strict with you.

THEODOSIA: You had to be. You know I'm bad. You couldn't do nothin else, with me.

MOSES: You bring a child up soft and it grows frightened of its own shadow. Your mum was like that. Not strong enough to handle the fever when it come. So whenever you stepped out of line I slapped you, like I would a chavi.

THEODOSIA: It ain't the slaps that hurt, it's the silence.

MOSES: Never did know what she saw in me. She loved children. So wanted'em she did.

THEODOSIA: And the one she had, killed her.

MOSES: Don't you ever say that again! I don't blame you. It was me, I'm the one all along. Where was I when she called out to me? Where was I when she was dyin in the squalor of these compounds? Where was I for the burnin of the wagon? Fightin for the bastards that put us here, that's where I was. I didn't even get to say goodbye to her. It was me, not you. It was me. Me and the Gadjes of the forest that killed her.

He pulls her tighter to him still.

MOSES: Baby I won't hit you again. I swear I won't hit you ever again. May the Lord strike me down dead if I do.

He carries on rocking her as

The light slowly fades.

Act 2 Scene 4

The following evening.

Gypsy compound.

The snow has stopped falling. Lights come up on Moses who is awake, and lying on his bed in the tent. Theodosia sits on the barrel close by him, platting her hair. Fireworks can be heard going off in the background, intermittently lighting up the night sky

THEODOSIA: I was just thinking about how it'll be in the forest when all the Traveller's are gone.

MOSES: I'm glad I won't be here to see it.

THEODOSIA: You really don't wanna stay?

MOSES: It's time to go.

THEODOSIA: What will you miss most?

MOSES: The sound of Gypsy voices comin through the trees. Men talking together after a hard days work, children laughin and playin about, their mother's callin em in for a wash before bedtime. And I'll miss seein the horse's gallopin down the roads, the fires lightin up the darkness and the smoke in the lanes.

Pause.

THEODOSIA: Listen, can't you hear it? Shut your eyes and listen.

Reluctantly he shuts his eyes.

THEODOSIA: What can you hear?

MOSES: Fireworks.

THEODOSIA: No, listen harder. I can hear Romani hearts beatin as one with the forest. Because its wind is our breath, its streams our blood, and its silence, our truth. And it always will be. No matter where we are.

MOSES: Cos the forest knows our longin, regrets nothin, and whispers no goodbyes.

She turns to him in shock.

THEODOSIA: You know it. You know her poem.

MOSES: I never forgot a single word your mother said.

After a moment she gets up and moves out of the tent, towards the sound of the fireworks.

Will enters. Theodosia watches him for a long moment before looking away. Moses comes out of the tent to face him. Both men are wary of each other. Will reaches out his hand. Moses tentatively shakes it. Will gestures at the fireworks.

WILL: Remind you of anything, Moses?

MOSES: Don't seem that long ago the explosions were for real.

MOSES: Your missus was right. They didn't come to shift us today.

WILL: You're still packed up.

MOSES: We're moving in the mornin.

Will sneaks a glance at Theodosia.

WILL: The council's going to give you till early in the New Year if you want to stay. At least you'll have somewhere for Christmas.

THEODOSIA: We don't belong here any more.

WILL: Then where?

MOSES: We'll go up country for a while. Not like you to come here at night?

WILL: The forestry have asked me to do some work at Ringwood for the next few weeks. I came to tell you I wouldn't be around this way anymore, even if you were staying. And I know you're liable to pack up any minute and move without saying goodbye so I thought I'd drop by just in case. I'm glad I did.

MOSES: Come in the tent.

WILL: To be honest I haven't got a lot of time. I'm going to pick one or two things up from the cabin and head home. I won't be coming back this way so if I don't see you again, I... It's been more than good to know you.

MOSES: Nobody's been a better man to Travellers around here than you, Will. No man's been a better friend to us.

Both men shake hands again and the strong eye contact of friendship says more than words could. Will turns to Theodosia, but she doesn't return his look. He forces a smile then turns away.

Will exits.

Lights fade out.

Act 2 Scene 5

Later that night.

Outside Foresters cabin.

Will stands in a clearing in the trees a short distance from the cabin. Exploding fireworks can be heard and flashes seen in the night sky. He looks awkward, unsure of himself. After a while he hears a sound, then Theodosia enters.

THEODOSIA: Thought you'd be waitin inside the cabin.

WILL: I didn't think you'd want to come in.

She seems relaxed and in control. They stand apart.

WILL: Hope you didn't mind me coming to the camp. I thought about it long and hard. But I had to see you again.

THEODOSIA: What for?

WILL: Try to explain.

THEODOSIA: It's clear enough.

WILL: But I wanted to...

THEODOSIA: It's over. It's done.

He looks at the scene around him.

WILL: The forest already seems different. Empty somehow. I noticed it as I walked up here. It's as if the sprit of the place has...

THEODOSIA: Gilo asa bavolengro adrey o rarde.

WILL: Yes. Gone like a ghost in the night.

He watches her as she stares out into the distance.

WILL: I owe you so much.

THEODOSIA: You owe me nothin.

WILL: I see things differently because of you.

THEODOSIA: Tute are corredo. You see nothin.

Beat

WILL: I'm honoured you'll at least leave me your language.

THEODOSIA: Yeah. You'll have my people's words to remember us by.

She pulls her coat tightly around her.

THEODOSIA: I told mi dad I wouldn't be long.

WILL: He looked different tonight. I thought he might be in fighting mood but he was more... I don't know, easy somehow.

THEODOSIA: He's gonna be all right. We talked. Opened the wound and cleaned out the poison. It'll heal now. Take time but it will. All I had to do was stand up to him. Though it probably helped to have two people do it in one day.

WILL: I softened him up for you?

THEODOSIA: He'd have killed you in the end.

He smiles. She doesn't return it.

THEODOSIA: She knows you're here, don't she?

WILL: Yes.

THEODOSIA: How can you live like it Will? Without love, without passion?

WILL: I'm happy enough.

THEODOSIA: Are you?

WILL: It's my choice and I've made it. I'll learn to live with it. Life isn't a poem, Dosia. Sometimes it doesn't sound nice or rhyme.

THEODOSIA: Poems don't have to rhyme or sound nice. Just be true.

WILL: I'm not like you. I'm not a Gypsy, I know that now. I want roots and there's a price to pay for them.

THEODOSIA: You're livin a lie.

WILL: I don't expect you to understand.

THEODOSIA: You're wrong. When you walked away from me after the fight and went with her I saw you for the first time. And I understood. I feel sorry for both of you.

WILL: The time you and I have had together, especially the last few weeks…You know what you've meant to me. I don't regret anything.

THEODOSIA: I do. I regret believin. Our cultures despise each other so why did I think we could be any different?

WILL: Is that what you think it's come to for us?

84

THEODOSIA: I'll never hate you. But look where love has got us.

She walks downstage centre and looks out as if to the village and fireworks below.

THEODOSIA: I've grown into a woman with you. Feels like a twisted kind of freedom. Mi insides've come apart. It's like I'm made of water, like there's no blood left in mi veins. Mi skin's empty.

She glances across at him.

THEODOSIA: But it won't be for long. I know that now.

She turns away.

THEODOSIA: I'm leavin mi dad.

He's surprised at the news.

THEODOSIA: Goin to live with mi grandmother.

WILL: For how long?

THEODOSIA: A year or so.

WILL: Does he know?

THEODOSIA: I'll tell him when we get away from here. It'll do him good in the end. Might even find he's self a woman with me out the way. Takin a mort'd be chusti for him at this time in his life. But I don't suppose he will.

WILL: Are you ever coming back here?

THEODOSIA: Might do. But I doubt it.

WILL: I hope things...I don't know. Get better for your people, for Travellers. Hope my lot will learn to give you a chance.

THEODOSIA: Nobody's gonna give us anythin. We've got to take it. We need to learn to speak up for ourselves. Tell people who we are, what we want and stand our ground till we get it.

WILL: And your mother's poetry, will you ever learn to read and write so you can put it down?

She thinks carefully about the question.

THEODOSIA: Yeah. I think I will.

She takes in a lungful of cold night air then lets it out.

THEODOSIA: Tonight feels like one life is over and another's beginnin for me. And if there's a God in Heaven, I'll swear to it, nobody's ever gonna take this one away from me. Not mi father, not you, not my people, or yours. It's gonna be mine. Because I have somethin in me now that's bigger and means more than any of us. The one real thing that's come out of all this.

He looks at her quizzically.

THEODOSIA: I've made up a poem of my own about it. Wanna hear it?

He nods, slightly unsure. She puts her hands in her coat pockets and stands square and strong.

THEODOSIA: Unclean is what I am. Contaminated with the blood of a Gadje in my veins. Curst and cast out by my people when they discover their traitress. *She smiles.* So why has joy exploded in me? Because he has planted in my womb a deep song that I will sing forever.

Silence, apart from the explosions in the background. He watches her, stunned. She turns to him.

THEODOSIA: Do you like it?

He studies her closely, trying to work out if she's serious.

THEODOSIA: Don't worry Will, I can keep a secret. If I get buried when I die, they'll put it on my gravestone. "Here lies Theodosia Hilldon; no one knew her secrets".

She takes a step away from him and adds as an afterthought, as if to herself.

THEODOSIA: "No one knew her pain."

She takes a final look around.

THEODOSIA: It's gonna be a hard winter all right. But the ice'll melt in the end. Always does.

He still can't find the words. She shivers against the cold.

THEODOSIA: I know it's cold, but don't the forest look magical covered in snow?

WILL: Theodosia…

THEODOSIA: *With finality.* We've had our chance.

She stands back and takes in the sight of the exploding fireworks.

THEODOSIA: I love fireworks. Don't you?

She exits. He slowly moves stage left and sits down on a tree stump. After a moment he puts his head in his hands.

The lights fade to black.

The Gamekeeper
by
Josephine Carter

First performance 22nd February 2007 Hale Village Hall

Characters and doubling (original cast and production team)

Frank – Roger Butcher
Sally – Ruth Dawes
Jenni – Ebony Feare
Stage Manager – Dominic Phillips
Director – David Haworth
Designer – Helen Goddard

Act 1 Scene1

*The set consists of a very old-fashioned and basic
room. It is the living room of a gamekeeper's cottage. Upstage
left there is door leading outside. There is a table and couple
of chairs, a kitchen cupboard and old calor gas cooker. A
sagging armchair is beside a wood-burning stove, and upstage
is a dresser with a small amount of crockery, but mainly filled
with books. Stage right is a lean-to section added at a later
date, housing a sink, and a door to the toilet. Stage left is a
door to the only other room, used as a bedroom. When the
curtain rises the stage is in darkness except for a glow from the
wood stove. There is the sound of the back door opening and
we see the shape of someone quietly easing themselves into the
main room. The shape moves towards the stove, when suddenly
it stumbles and there is a splash.*

JENNI: Shit!!

*After a moment the door from the bedroom flings open and the
shaft of light reveals Frank standing there with a shotgun, it
also reveals Jenni, spread-eagled in a tin bath.*

JENNI: Oh my God!

FRANK: Get out.

JENNI: I can't.

FRANK: Out! I'm not telling you again.

JENNI: I'm stuck.

FRANK: I'll put the dog on you.

JENNI: You blind or somethin'? I'm Stuck!

Frank switches on the light and Jenni immediately reacts to the sight of the gun.

JENNI: Jeez! Don't use that mister.

FRANK: Why not?

JENNI: I didn't mean nothin'.

FRANK: You meant no good, else you wouldn't be here.

He takes a step forward.

JENNI: Don't shoot!

FRANK: *Putting gun to one side.* No. Bullet be wasted on such a wet piece of trash.

JENNI: I ain't trash.

She struggles to get out.

FRANK: What you doing here?

JENNI: Sitting in freezin' water. Where's the dog?

FRANK: What?

JENNI: Where's the bleedin' dog?

FRANK: There's no dog. Come on, move!

Jenni struggles and then holds out her hand. Frank pulls her out of the bath and she stands dripping and shivering. Sighing, Frank turns and picks up the gun.

JENNI: No!

FRANK: Don't worry I don't need a gun to deal with the likes of you.

He moves across to the cupboard and gets out a towel, which he hands to Jenni, and then goes into the bedroom. Jenni wraps the towel round herself. After a moment or two Frank returns with an old pair of trousers and a jumper.

FRANK: For God's sake girl; you'll have to strip to dry yourself.

JENNI: I ain't stripping.

FRANK: Go in there and put these on while your clothes dry and I decide what to do with you. *He pulls the bath to one side and then gets a cloth and mops the floor.* You've made a right mess here.

JENNI: *Offstage.* What's it doing there?

FRANK: Had a bath didn't I? Couldn't throw it out or I'd be skating tomorrow. More to the point what are you doing here?

JENNI: What d'you mean?

FRANK: Simple enough question. What are you doing in my...

JENNI: I mean about the skating.

FRANK: It's freezing. The path would be a sheet of ice in the morning.

JENNI: Oh. Ain't you got no bathroom?

FRANK: There's the sink, but I don't quite fit. Just answer the question girl, what you doing breaking in?

JENNI: I didn't, door was open.

FRANK: No it wasn't. Mightn't have been locked but it weren't open.

JENNI: Yeah, well I didn't break in.

FRANK: You weren't invited.

JENNI: What? Oh yeah, but it's cold enough to freeze your balls off out there.

FRANK: Which you shouldn't know anything about.

JENNI: I know all about them.

FRANK: Well you shouldn't. You're too young.

JENNI: Too young?

FRANK: How old are you?

JENNI: Er. Eighteen.

FRANK: And I'm the King of Siam. You're no more than twelve.

JENNI: I'm fourteen O.K? What's it matter?

FRANK: It matters because you're in my house in the middle of the night. Your mum'll be worried sick.

JENNI: She couldn't care a toss.

FRANK: So that's it; a family tiff?

JENNI: Yeah, a tiff.

She shivers.

FRANK: Oh for God's sake.

He pulls out a stool from under the table for her to sit in front of the fire. He finds some glasses and a bottle of whisky and pours a small tot for her and a larger one for himself.

FRANK: Where you from?

JENNI: London.

FRANK: Whereabouts?

JENNI: Er...the East End.

FRANK: Don't believe you. Where are you headed?

JENNI: Southampton.

FRANK: Well the nearest road to Southampton from here is from Newbury. *Silence.* So you're from Newbury.

JENNI: Who says?

FRANK: I do.

Hands her the whisky.

JENNI: What's this?

FRANK: Whisky. I can't stand the sight of you sitting there shivering like a frightened rabbit.

JENNI: I'm freezin'.

FRANK: It's the middle of winter. Drink that up, you'll need something inside to warm you.

JENNI: What for?

FRANK: As you have pointed out, it's cold outside.

JENNI: You saying I've got to go?

FRANK: Yes

JENNI: Can't I stay ?

FRANK: You've got a cheek. *Looks out of window.* Still I suppose I wouldn't turn the rats out on a night like this.

JENNI: You got rats here?

FRANK: If I can't keep a silly scrap of a girl out I certainly can't rats.

JENNI: I can't stand rats.

FRANK: Ever seen one? *Jenni shakes her head.* Then you don't know what you're talking about. They're not hungry so you've nothing to worry about. What's your name?

JENNI: Jenni. Jenni, er…Smith.

FRANK: Oh well a half-truth is better than an outright lie. We'll decide what to do with you tomorrow. You'll have to sleep in the chair.

JENNI: Er, thanks.

FRANK: There's nothing worth stealing but don't go poking about.

JENNI: I won't. Promise.

FRANK: Is that worth anything? *He goes into the bedroom and returns with a blanket which he hands to Jenni.* Here. I don't know how you found me in the first place.

JENNI: Dunno. P'raps I've got a Guardian Angel.

FRANK: Lucky girl. I could do with one of those.

He exits into bedroom and closes the door. Now alone Jenni goes to the dresser and is about to open a drawer but then decides against it. She wraps herself in the blanket and settles in the chair. Blackout

Scene 2

Jenni is curled up uncomfortably in the chair. Frank is at the stove. Jenni stirs.

FRANK: Come on girl. Time you was up and about.

JENNI: It's morning?

FRANK: It's nine o'clock, practically the afternoon.

JENNI: *Easing herself out of the chair.* Ouch.

FRANK: Should've stayed at home in your own bed.

JENNI: No, it was great. No noise or nothin'. What's that?

FRANK: Porridge.

JENNI: It looks disgusting.

FRANK: But tastes better.

JENNI: I'm not eating that muck.

FRANK: Suit yourself. There's no call for me to feed you.

JENNI: And I never bleedin' well asked.

FRANK: And stop swearing.

JENNI: What?

FRANK: Don't swear. It's...unbecoming.

JENNI: Oh get real.

FRANK: I'm of an age that doesn't like to hear girls swear.

JENNI: Yeah, the dinosaur age.

FRANK: After breakfast we'll go down to the village and ring your mum.

JENNI: She's not on the 'phone.

FRANK: The police then. They'll send a message to her. She'll be fretting.

JENNI: Not her.

FRANK: Your dad then.

JENNI: He's long gone.

FRANK: Even more reason for your mum to be worried.

JENNI: She told me to go.

FRANK: You just had a row.

JENNI: O.K. I'll go, but I ain't 'phoning no-one.

FRANK: Where do you reckon to go?

JENNI: Told you. Southampton.

FRANK: You can't go traipsing around on your own. There's fellas out there that'd. That'd do you no good at all.

JENNI: I'd kick 'im in the where it hurts first.

FRANK: That's easier said than done.

JENNI: I can look after myself.

FRANK: Take last night for instance, many a man would've taken advantage.

JENNI: You? Get real Grandad!

FRANK: You're the one that should get real. You don't know where you're going, what you're doing. Go home girl.

JENNI: Ain't got no home.

FRANK: I thought you said...

There is a knock on the door, which immediately opens and a post-woman starts to come in, Frank tries to block her but without success.

SAL: Don't stand in the way Frank.

FRANK: Don't bother to wait for an invite will you?

SAL: It's freezing out there. Got the kettle on?

FRANK: You're not stopping are you?

SAL: What a welcome. Got out the wrong side of bed did we?

FRANK: No. Just wasn't expecting you.

SAL: Well is there tea or not?

FRANK: Er....yes, of course. Kettle's on.

SAL: You get a letter once in a blue moon, trust you to have one today when I can't even... *Seeing Jenni.* Oh! Hallo.

JENNI: Hallo.

FRANK: It could've waited.

SAL: What?

FRANK: The letter, it could've waited.

SAL: Oh no, I'm not allowed to sit on Her Majesty's mail just because it looks like snow. *Pause.* You going to introduce me Frank?

FRANK: What?

SAL: Your visitor.   An introduction would be nice.

FRANK: Oh...er...yes...well this young lady arrived late and...

JENNI: I'm his granddaughter. Lizzie.

SAL: Granddaughter? Well you kept that dark Frank.

FRANK: She's nothing of the sort, she's...*Looks at Jenni and then Sal, flounders and panics.* She's...er...she's my brother's granddaughter.

SAL: Your brother?   I didn't...

FRANK: So I'm really a great uncle. But that makes me sound like I'm a hundred and two.

JENNI: And he's a couple of years off that.

FRANK: Go and change your clothes

Jenni exits into bedroom.

SAL: And there I've known you forty odd years and it's the first I've heard of a brother.

FRANK: We're not that close.

SAL: Close enough to send his granddaughter to stay.

FRANK: Well. Er. Bit of a family upset I gather. I haven't got the full story yet.

SAL: But why didn't you ever...

FRANK: *Busying himself at the stove.* Right. Tea for us, porridge for...the lass.

SAL: Here's your letter.

FRANK: Looks like a bill.

Tosses it aside.

SAL: You know it's not.

FRANK: All the same, you needn't have bothered.

SAL: That's gratitude for you and I had to leave my bike at the bottom of the track, it's that slippery.

FRANK: Do you good. Get some of the fat off.

SAL: Cheeky. Anyway if it wasn't today I don't know when you'd have got it. There's worse to come.

FRANK: Looks like it. *Handing her tea.* Here.

SAL: Aren't you going to open it?

FRANK: No,

SAL: You don't know what's in it.

FRANK: I've got a pretty good idea.

SAL: And I thought you'd be anxious to know.

FRANK: Well I'm not.

SAL: Can't this brother of yours help?

FRANK: I told you, we're not close.

SAL: Blood's thicker than water.

FRANK: Leave it Sal. I'll sort it.

Jenni re-enters in her own clothes.

SAL: Well that looks better. Why on earth...?

FRANK: She got a bit wet last night.

SAL: Oh? Was it raining?

FRANK: D'you know this girl's never had porridge? Staple diet of the Scots and grand for a cold winter's morning. They eat it with salt but I think a dollop of treacle'll suit you better. *He serves it up.* Don't just look at it, eat it.

JENNI: *Tasting a little.* It's quite nice.

FRANK: Warming. Just what you need.

SAL: Where you from luv?

JENNI: London.

SAL: Whereabouts?

JENNI: East End.

SAL: That's a bit vague. I've got a cousin runs a pub at West Ham, King's Head. That anywhere near you?

JENNI: I don't go to pubs.

FRANK: That's a daft question Sal. It's like her asking if you know someone who lives near an oak tree.

SAL: Just being friendly.

FRANK: Have you ever been to London?

104

SAL: Went on a W.I. outing once to the Royal Tournament.

FRANK: I expect you passed a pub or two on the way.

SAL: Ooh, forgive me for breathing.

FRANK: Sorry. I'm a bit tetchy what with this scrap arriving out of the blue.

SAL: How did you get here luv?

JENNI: I walked.

SAL: From Brockenhurst station? But that's five miles at least.

FRANK: Taxi to the village. Sounds like the inquisition here.

SAL: Oops. Slapped wrist again. Born nosy, that's me,

FRANK: Hate to rush you Sal, but if bad weather's on its way I'd better go and get some provisions.

SAL: If you've got a list I'll drop it in the shop so they've got it ready for you.

FRANK: No, don't worry. Got to change things a bit what with er...

SAL: O.K. Take care. 'Bye. Um?

JENNI: Lizzie.

SAL: Oh yes. 'Bye then Lizzie.

FRANK: Thanks Sal. 'Bye.

Sally exits.

JENNI: She didn't believe us.

FRANK: Not surprised with me suddenly acquiring all these relatives.

JENNI: There's only me.

FRANK: No. She knows I haven't got any children, but now I've got a brother who must have had a wife, to get himself a child, who also must have a wife or husband to get you.

JENNI: They didn't have to be married. *Frank sighs.* Anyway why would she know? She's only a post-woman.

FRANK: She's an old friend who happens to be the post-woman. As she said we go back a long way.

JENNI: Oh.

FRANK: Come on, finish your breakfast and we'll be off.

JENNI: Where?

FRANK: Down to see Jim Dodds, he's the local copper. We can tell him all about it and he can get in touch with your mum.

JENNI: Can't I stay here for a bit?

FRANK: No.

106

JENNI: Why not?

FRANK: I don't want you.

JENNI: I thought you'd let me.

FRANK: Well I won't...the implications. Oh, finish your breakfast. I'm going to get some logs in.

He exits. Jenni, uncertain for a moment she looks around, there is a cry from outside which she ignores. She grabs an old coat and puts it on. She's hurrying now, pulling out drawers looking in pots for money. She finds some in a pot, makes to pocket it all, then puts half back. She goes to the door and opens it, Frank is lying there, hand raised to knock on the door. She stops for a moment then steps over him and starts up the path.

FRANK: Bloody little bitch!

He starts to pull himself into the house as he does so Jenni stops, turns and comes back to him.

JENNI: What d'you call me?

FRANK: You heard.

JENNI: Yeah I did. You're all mouth ain't you. " Don't swear, it ain't becoming." Well it ain't becoming for an old man neither and I ain't no bitch. D'you hear me?!

FRANK: I've hurt my leg not my ears.

JENNI: What?

FRANK: Don't shout.

JENNI: I'll bleedin' well shout if I want to.

FRANK: Don't! Go, just go. *Jenni stands looking down at him.* At least get out of the way.

JENNI: D'you want help?

FRANK: Just help me get inside.

JENNI: *Grabbing him by the shoulders, she pulls him part way inside.* Can you sit up?

Frank turns over and levers himself into a sitting position.

FRANK: And shut the door.

JENNI: *Swivels his legs away from the doorway and shuts the door.* What's wrong with your leg then, you broke it?

FRANK: Sprained my ankle I think, and done my back in.

They stagger to the chair. She takes the poker and stirs the fire.

FRANK: I dropped the wood outside. *Jenni goes to the door.* Take care.

JENNI: What?

FRANK: Take care. We don't want two crocks.

108

JENNI: Oh. *She goes out and Frank notes the pot on the table. Jenni returns a few moments later dragging a full log basket. She puts a couple of logs on the stove.* That right?

FRANK: Fine thanks. Helped yourself to my coat I see.

JENNI: You got others.

FRANK: You could've asked.

JENNI: Would you have given it me?

FRANK: I don't know. Anyway it wasn't only the coat was it?

JENNI: I didn't take it all.

FRANK: That's not thieving then? Not taking it all.

JENNI: I need it. I ain't got any.

FRANK: And I live on air?

JENNI: Well you've got more ain't you? Stashed away.

FRANK: No.

JENNI: I've got to get to Southampton. I'll send it back when I've earned some.

FRANK: You're going then?

JENNI: D'you want me to stay?

FRANK: Why should I?

JENNI: Right then I'll go now.

FRANK: Don't get lost.

JENNI: I got here didn't I?

FRANK: More by luck than judgement.

JENNI: What?

FRANK: Nothing.

JENNI: 'Bye then...thanks.

FRANK: It's going to snow.

JENNI: I've seen snow.

FRANK: I remember in seventy three, when it hit the South Coast. Haven't seen anything like it since.

JENNI: What you saying?

FRANK: Going to happen again I reckon.

JENNI: Better get on the road then.

FRANK: You going to 'phone?

JENNI: *Opening door.* No.

FRANK: Think of your mum.

JENNI: She don't care.

110

FRANK: You don't know.

JENNI: And you don't...not the half of it. *She hesitates.* 'Bye.

FRANK: Jenni.

JENNI: Yeah?

FRANK: You...you could stay...for a day or two. *She looks back at him. He indicates his leg.* I could do with some help.

JENNI: What about the swearing then?

FRANK: I'd rather you didn't.

JENNI: *Trying not to look relieved she shuts the door.* O.K. then. *She slumps down at the table and looks around.* Ain't you got no TV?

FRANK: No. I live in splendid isolation.

JENNI: What?

FRANK: No television, no radio, no telephone.

JENNI: Why?

FRANK: I prefer my own company.

JENNI: Oh.What d'you do then?

FRANK: I walk, work in the garden, I grow my own vegetables, I read a lot.

JENNI: Jeeze. Bloody borin'.

FRANK: Do you think you could help me?

JENNI: What? Oh yeah. What d'you want me to do?

FRANK: Look in that cupboard. You'll find an old sheet or towel we can tear up to bandage my ankle.

She finds an old sheet, Frank rips it up, she takes off his boot and between them they bandage his ankle.

JENNI: Your sock stinks.

FRANK: Yes, I'm sorry about that. I wasn't expecting a nurse to call.

JENNI: What's the point in 'aving a bath and puttin' on smelly socks?

FRANK: Point taken.

JENNI: What would you've done if I hadn't been here?

FRANK: I'd have managed.

JENNI: How?

FRANK: Crawled.

JENNI: You couldn't have reached the cupboard.

FRANK: Perhaps not.

JENNI: Perhaps!

FRANK: Yes. Well. I'd have managed, I'd have had to.   Good pull as tight as you can, now wind it back up again and I'll tie it off.

JENNI: D'you want the stool?

FRANK: Thanks.

JENNI: You going to take the other stinkin' sock off?

FRANK: Yes, O.K. *He struggles with the other boot and sock as Jenni watches.* There might be some more in there.

JENNI: *Returning with the socks.* Found them.
And…*Produces a bundle of notes from behind her back.*
You're a liar old man.

FRANK: And you're a thief girl.

Pause

JENNI: I'll put it back.

FRANK: No give it here.

JENNI: You alright?

FRANK: No. My leg hurts, my back hurts and I'm at the mercy of a little vixen.

JENNI: What's a vixen?

FRANK: A female fox, noted for being cunning and sly.

JENNI: You asked me to stay.

FRANK: Don't make me regret it then.

JENNI: D'you want a hot water bottle for your back? I saw one in the cupboard.

FRANK: Oh…thanks. *Jenni puts the kettle on and busies herself clearing the table as Frank watches, puzzled.* Do you make yourself as helpful as this at home?

JENNI: No fear.

FRANK: Why not?

JENNI: Have to go to school don't I?

FRANK: Do you like it?

JENNI: What? School? No, waste of time.

FRANK: Don't you believe it. Education…you'll never regret it.

JENNI: Did you like it?

FRANK: Different in my day. Basic three Rs and pulled out at twelve to work on the farm.

JENNI: Did you like working on a farm?

FRANK: Blooming hard work but I couldn't have done nine to five behind a desk. Better than the army too.

JENNI: Was you in the war?

FRANK: Just missed it. National Service.

JENNI: What's that?

FRANK: After the war you had to do two years in one of the services, Army, Navy or Air Force. Rules, regulations, shouted at morning noon and night. Glad to get out of that. Some said it was good for you. Maybe it was, didn't seem so at the time but it might straighten out some of the yobs we've got now.

JENNI: *Putting the bottle at his back.* That O.K?

FRANK: Fine thanks.

JENNI: D'you want some of your whisky?

FRANK: Yes, thanks. *Jenni pours some and brings it over.* This seems a sudden change of heart, why?

JENNI: I'm not sly.

FRANK: No?

JENNI: No. But even if you thought I was you still said 'take care'.

FRANK: What?

JENNI: No-one's ever said that. 'Watch it!' or 'Mind!' But that's not the same somehow as 'take care'.

FRANK: Powerful thing words. You've got to be careful how you use them.

JENNI: You didn't mean it then?

FRANK: I meant it.

JENNI: You ain't opened your letter.

FRANK: No.

JENNI: Don't you want it?

FRANK: Not really...oh, pass it over

Jenni does so and he reads it and then tosses it aside.

FRANK: The buggers. *He reaches for a book beside his chair. On looking at it he mutters to himself.* Oh, finished it.....um.. cold winter's day' Dickens I think. *Speaks to Jenni.* Would you get me down David Copperfield from the shelf? *Jenni ignores him.* Jenni!

JENNI: What?

FRANK: Would you get me a book from the shelf? David Copperfield, please.

Pause
JENNI: I dunno where it is.

FRANK: On the shelf.

JENNI: I'll help you stand.

FRANK: Don't be silly, it's over there, I know it is.

JENNI: *Looking along shelves.* Can't see it.

FRANK: It must be there, got a red cover I think.

Jenni picks up a red book and brings it over.

FRANK: No, this is The Mayor of Casterbridge. Thomas Hardy.

JENNI: You said it was red.

FRANK: I know but this plainly says on the spine 'The Mayor of...' *A thought strikes him and he looks at Jenni for a moment or two.* I'm sorry, perhaps it's not red. But its David Copperfield I want. By Charles Dickens.

JENNI: I done your bleedin' leg up, what else do you want?

FRANK: Just a book.

She stomps over to the bookcase and brings back several books.

JENNI: 'Ere. Make up your mind.

FRANK: Here it is. My mistake, brown cover. Do you need glasses?

JENNI: No.

FRANK: It's just that the title is on the spine.

JENNI: You said it was red.

FRANK: I know, but it is quite clear, David Copperfield.

JENNI: Don't go on about it. The writing's different, not like at school.

FRANK: The print's a little old fashioned that's all. Can't you read?

JENNI: 'Course I can.

FRANK: But not very well. What the hell do you do at your school if they don't teach you to read?

JENNI: Don't shout at me. You've no right to shout at me. I can read school books.

FRANK: Sorry. How can you read your school books and not this?

JENNI: Well, I know what they say.

FRANK: What do you mean?

JENNI: I hear the others read and I remember what they say.

FRANK: That's terrible.

JENNI: No it ain't.

FRANK: Yes it is. Someone should have cottoned on to what you were doing. Why do you do it? Didn't you learn your alphabet when you were a little girl?

JENNI: 'Corse I did, I 'aint stupid ...A,B,C.D...

FRANK: O.K, O.K. but...

JENNI: I just listen...

FRANK: And remember. Clever but foolish. But there must be some classes where things aren't read aloud and you have to...

JENNI: I skip them.

FRANK: What does your mum say about that?

JENNI: She don't care. She can't read any rate.

FRANK: But I thought it was the law that parents had to make their children attend school.

JENNI: How they going to do that?

FRANK: Your mother would be fined if you missed too many lessons.

JENNI: Cor! The shit'd really hit the fan then.

FRANK: Don't you care?
JENNI: No.

FRANK: What are you good at?

JENNI: I like playing the recorder.

FRANK: You can read music then?

JENNI: Well that's just dots ain't it? In different places.

FRANK: I suppose so. I can't read music.

JENNI: And drawing, I like drawing.

FRANK: Draw something for me then. *He gives her the envelope.* Here on the back of this.

JENNI: No.

FRANK: Why not?

JENNI: Don't want to.

FRANK: You said you could draw; prove it.

JENNI: Haven't got nothin' to draw with.

FRANK: There'll be a pencil on the shelf somewhere.

Jenni finds a pencil and settles herself at the table and Frank sits and ponders for a moment or two.

FRANK: You must learn to read.

JENNI: What for?

FRANK: There's books, papers, magazines. Stories, information, news...everything.

JENNI: It's on the tele.

FRANK: What if you haven't got one?

JENNI: It's only nutters like you that ain't.

FRANK: But there's so much the television can't do. People have been writing for hundreds of years.

JENNI: They didn't have no tele or video.

FRANK: You can draw. That's different from the T.V. Special. Reading is pictures in your mind.

Jenni finishes her drawing and hands it to him

JENNI: It ain't a proper drawing. I mean I ain't put in all the details yet. D'you know what it is?

FRANK: Oh yes. It's an old man, me, sitting by the fire. It's very good, in fact it's excellent. If you can draw you can write, writing's only drawing shapes for letters and if you can write you can read.

JENNI: Teachers said I was too lazy and stupid.

FRANK: No you're not, and going through life without reading, why its like...it'd be worse than going through life without love.
JENNI: That ain't so hard.

FRANK: Oh come on. No boyfriend? And despite what you say your mother loves you.

JENNI: The only person she loves is her bleedin' boyfriend and I know that 'cos she told me. So just shut it, you don't know nothing about it.

Scene 3

The stage is dark although there is a faint light from outside and a glow from the stove, and we can just make out Frank's shape asleep in the chair. Moonlight starts to stream in as clouds pass, Frank wakes, struggles to his feet, and goes to look out of the window.

FRANK: You little bugger!

There's a yell from the bedroom and Jenni comes dashing in.

JENNI: It's the Pigs. Don't let them find me, please Frank, please!

FRANK: What you talking about girl? It was a fox and your yelling's frightened her off.

JENNI: The lights! They've come looking for me.

FRANK: Its the moonlight on the snow, makes it bright as day. Come here and have a look. There!

JENNI: Ooh! I thought it was headlights.

FRANK: And you thought it was the coppers come to haul you off. This isn't some B movie where they chase the villains through all weathers. Old Jim Dodds is going to stay tucked up in his bed for some while yet no matter what you've done...and what have you done?

JENNI: Me? Nothing. I ain't done nothing.

FRANK: No?

JENNI: No. Look, there's marks in the snow, someone is out there.

FRANK: No, that was the fox. We left the shed door open and she stole the rabbit that was going to be tomorrow's lunch. I told you they were cunning.

JENNI: A rabbit! You was keeping a rabbit in the shed?

FRANK: Best place, nice and cold. It was dead, shot it yesterday morning.

JENNI: And you were going to eat it!

FRANK: No other use for a dead rabbit.

JENNI: Ugh!

FRANK: Don't be stupid girl. What you think you eat? Your sausages and hamburgers were all pigs or cows once, with skin, innards and horns. You knew that, you're not stupid.

JENNI: Don't like to think 'bout it.
FRANK: Well hop back to bed before you freeze to death.

JENNI: D'you want to go back to your chair?

FRANK: No. I'll wait for the dawn. A clear sky, it'll be a rare sight this morning.

JENNI: Is it morning?

FRANK: Not far off.

JENNI: What's happened to the lights?

FRANK: Line'll be down. It was a heavy fall. There's an oil lamp under the sink.

Jenni re-enters having put on her trainers and struggling into Frank's coat.

JENNI: Oil lamp?

FRANK: In the cupboard under the sink. Bring it here, I've matches in my pocket.

JENNI: *Gets the lamp.* I've never seen one of these.

FRANK: We have a lot of cuts here. Put some wood on the fire and then make some tea. *Jenni puts the kettle on and stokes the fire.* Bring the rug over will you? I could do with it round my shoulders and you can put this on the table.

JENNI: *Obeying all commands.* I'm not your bloody skivvy you know.

FRANK: You're not my granddaughter either. Make the tea girl and then come and see something magical. *Jenni busies herself and Frank stands in silence for a moment or two.* Why don't you sleep through?

JENNI: What?

FRANK: You were surprised you'd slept all night, why?

JENNI: I wake up.

FRANK: Why?

JENNI: I get woken by noises. Him creepin' about.

FRANK: Who?

JENNI: Mum's fella.

FRANK: Comes in late does he?

JENNI: Comes in drunk more like.

FRANK: Falls up the stairs does he?

JENNI: And some.

FRANK: What? *Jenni shrugs.* What?

JENNI: *Brings the tea over and gives Frank a cup.* Forget it.

They drink their tea in silence.

JENNI: It don't look like the snow we get at home.

FRANK: Well it doesn't get mucked up with traffic but here it's marvellous. You forget its harshness burying food and livestock. But look at it girl. The moonlight, sparkle, shadows, it's magical don't you think?

JENNI: It's cool.

FRANK: *Laughing.* It is that. This is why I live here. The peace, the beauty and the honesty, what you see is what you get, no side...and sleeping through.

JENNI: Don't you get lonely?

FRANK: Never. I've all the company I want, birds, animals, trees.

JENNI: But no people.

FRANK: No, thank God, but you do need to be a special kind of person to live here, independent, selfish, cantankerous. It's not for a lively young girl who has a life before her and a loving mum at home worrying herself silly.

JENNI: Not her, the only person she loves is that creep. *Pause.* It is like magic ain't it? *She gazes out the window, entranced. Frank hesitates then puts a hand on her shoulder. She immediately shakes him off.* Sod off!

Blackout

Scene 4

It is about midday and Frank has just made a pot of tea when something catches his attention and he goes to look out of the window.

FRANK: Bloody hell! *He goes and opens the door.* What the blazes are you doing woman? Come in.

Sal enters with a loaded rucksack.

SAL: That's a nice welcome after I've risked life and limb.

FRANK: I doubt that. I mean it doesn't look as though you've got the National winner out there. Whose horse is it? I didn't know you could ride.

SAL: Bill Powers' and you don't need to know all my secrets. Dad used to deliver the mail on horseback.

FRANK: You're not going to tell me you struggled up on that nag just to deliver me another letter from the council.

SAL: No. I was worried about you.

FRANK: What for?

SAL: Aren't you going to offer a frozen post-woman a cuppa?

FRANK: Just brewed. *As they talk he pours two mugs of tea and they drink.* You didn't answer. Why on earth were you worried?

SAL: You said you were coming down to the village for some stores. I was chatting to Nancy this morning and she said you hadn't been in, so I thought I'd better bring something up and see what had happened.

FRANK: Nothing happened.

SAL: Why are you limping then?

FRANK: I just twisted my ankle. Anyway I've always got plenty of tins as a standby.

SAL: I'd better have a look at it.

FRANK: It's O.K. The lass helped.

SAL: Oh whatshername, your great niece is still here then?

FRANK: Of course.

SAL: This is foul. At least I'll have some proper milk in this tea instead of that disgusting powder as I've taken the trouble to bring it up. *She pours her tea down the sink and pours herself a fresh mug, then takes some milk out of her rucksack. Whilst talking she unpacks eggs, sausages, vegetable, fruit, etc. and puts them away; the cupboard is fairly empty.* Wheres all these standby tins then?

FRANK: We've been using them haven't we?

SAL: Why didn't you send her down to the village then?

FRANK: In this weather? She'd have got lost and then I would have been in trouble.

128

SAL: Not as much as you're headed for at the moment.

FRANK: What d'you mean?

SAL: On the TV last night there was a report on a missing girl.

FRANK: On the National news?

SAL: No, Meridian. A mother asking her runaway daughter to come home. Nothing to worry about, all is forgiven; that's what she said.

FRANK: Why are you telling me this?

SAL: You know why. *Frank looks at her, refusing to comment.* Where is she then, your great-niece?

FRANK: Chopping wood. I've got the first aid kit out as I'm fully expecting her to hack her foot off.

SAL: Nobody can do anything right except you can they?

FRANK: I'm not saying that, but a town kid hasn't got a vast experience of wood chopping.

SAL: Why didn't you tell me about her?

FRANK: I didn't know she existed.

SAL: About this brother then? You always said you were alone in the world.

FRANK: So I am.

SAL: With a brother?

FRANK: As you said, you don't need to know all my secrets.

SAL: Hiding a brother is a bit different to me forgetting to mention I could ride.

FRANK: It's not important. He left home before I did. Hardly kept in touch.

SAL: But why have you never told me? All the time we've known one another.

FRANK: I can't remember that we did that much talking.

SAL: I used to tell you things.

FRANK: Well that's you isn't it? I've never been that chatty.

SAL: You talked enough when you had your...difficulties.

FRANK: Difficulties! Oh Sal, you and your euphemisms.

SAL: Laugh away, but I was there for you wasn't I?

FRANK: Yes you were, and I was grateful.

SAL: Who's using euphemisms now? Is that what you call it, gratitude?

FRANK: Don't start getting uptight with me.

SAL: Why not? When you tell me our relationship was nothing to you but gratitude.

130

FRANK: That's not what I said. It was fun but it could never be much more than that. You had Phil and me...well you know me.

SAL: I'm wondering if I do.

FRANK: Anyway we're a bit past it now anyhow.

SAL: Speak for yourself.

FRANK: Sorry. You, of course, are just a chick compared to this old rooster.

SAL: But it's not a matter of being past it. I always thought it was something more than just a roll in the hay. Wasn't it?

FRANK: Of course it was. Look, have a whisky and we'll drink to old times. You've stocked me up on that I hope?

SAL: Would I dare forget? Yes I'll have a small tot. Are you sure there's nothing you want to tell me?

FRANK: No. I mean yes, I'm sure.

SAL: Well there's something I want to talk to you about.

FRANK: *He pours out two whiskies.* That sounds ominous.

SAL: You mentioned a letter from the council. Why don't you think about it Frank? No; let me finish. I went to look at the plans. You haven't done that have you?

FRANK: Because I'm not interested.

SAL: There's going to be a nice little courtyard garden, its very tasteful.

FRANK: Tasteful! What the hell do I want with tasteful? Let alone falling over old dears and their zimmer frames in the courtyard garden.

SAL: It won't be like that.

FRANK: How do you know? When the council say elderly, they mean incontinent and incompetent.

SAL: Well you were the one who said you were past it.

FRANK: I need my freedom.

SAL: It's not a prison. I'm talking about somewhere to live. Somewhere of your own.

FRANK: I don't want it. I don't need it.

SAL: But you will. As you've pointed out you're no spring chicken. You need people, friends, nearby.

FRANK: I don't. I've always been alone.

SAL: Not always.

FRANK: *Glaring.* Long enough. Let's change the subject shall we?

SAL: What if you'd broken your leg instead of twisting your ankle? What if Lizzie hadn't been here?

132

FRANK: Well I didn't, and she was. Anyway faithful postie rode up to the rescue on her charger.

SAL: She won't always.

FRANK: Perhaps I'll have some peace then.

Sal sighs in exasperation

FRANK: I'm sorry.

SAL: Really?

FRANK: I know I'm an old grouch.

SAL: I'm used to it. Anyway I know it's only a cover.

FRANK: For what?

SAL: For the old softie inside.

The moment becomes suddenly tender and just as Frank draws Sal towards him Jenni kicks the door open, her arms full of logs.

JENNI: Have you seen it? There's a bleeding…whoops! Sorry.

SAL: Hello dear. That's Beauty. I just bought some stores up before you both starved to death.

JENNI: Beauty! You got some imagination. She snarled at me.

FRANK: Horses don't snarl.

JENNI: This one did. Like this.

She bares her teeth and sticks her neck forward. Frank laughs.

SAL: She probably thought those logs were something to eat.

JENNI: She nearly got them at her head. Scared me shitless.

FRANK: You can put those by the fire. Is that all you've done?

JENNI: No. I've done a blee....great pile.

SAL: Frank was fully expecting you to chop your foot off.

JENNI: Told him I wouldn't. I'm not as stupid as he thinks.

SAL: Don't worry. He's like that with everyone.

JENNI: Not you.

SAL: Especially me.

JENNI: Well I better go and stack them logs like I was told.

She exits. After she has left Sal laughs.

FRANK: What?

SAL: Very tactful.

FRANK: What?

SAL: Leaving us on our own.

FRANK: Oh, rubbish.

SAL: We know that, but I think that's why she's gone out again, but...

FRANK: But what?

SAL: It's been three years since I lost Phil and...well I want more than friendship Frank.

FRANK: I can't do that. I've been a loner too long.

SAL: Anyway I'm giving up. They're enlarging the round, supplying a van. I don't drive and I don't want to learn.

FRANK: What'll you do?

SAL: Have a little more time for myself, take up a hobby, join a club, meet people, socially I mean.

FRANK: So you're on a manhunt than?

SAL: So what if I am?

FRANK: Your business. Anyway it'll be a damn sight more comfortable being rescued in a van than draped across an old nag.

SAL: Oh you!

She goes to collect his glass. He takes her hand. Jenni enters.

JENNI: Oops! Thought I'd given you enough time.

SAL: You have, I'm just off. And what about you?

JENNI: What d'you mean?

SAL: When are you going?

JENNI: Dunno.

SAL: Your family will be missing you.

JENNI: No they won't.

She exits into bedroom, taking off her jacket.

FRANK: I'll still see you?

SAL: You'll always been welcome when you come down to the village.

FRANK: Join in one of your social clubs? I don't think so.

SAL: Things change, they have to.

FRANK: Not for me.

SAL: They already have. *She indicates the bedroom.* And when you've sorted out that problem, what then?

FRANK: Back to normal.

SAL: Oh no. They'll have you out of here and by that time the flats will all be gone, and what'll you do then?

FRANK: I'll find out when it happens, if it happens.

SAL: It'll happen alright.

FRANK: Well, I can make a fresh start.

SAL: Doing what?

FRANK: Are you going?

SAL: Yes. *Calling.* 'Bye bye-Lizzie.

JENNI: *Off.* 'Bye.

FRANK: *Crosses to the window and watches her leave.* Christ!

He returns to the table and pours himself a large whisky which he downs in one gulp. Jenni has come in, and is watching him.

JENNI: You could've given her a quick one. I wouldn't have minded.

FRANK: What? My God girl, you've got a one-track mind. There's a time and place.

JENNI: She wanted to.

FRANK: No.

JENNI: You could call her back. I'll go and chop more wood.

FRANK: No!

JENNI: She knows about me.

FRANK: She suspects.

JENNI: So she'll tell 'cos she wants me out of the way.

FRANK: She may suspect but she doesn't know. *He grabs his gun and his coat and goes out.* She doesn't know anything and she won't say anything I can promise you that.

Blackout

Scene 5

The following day, Frank and Jenni are finishing a meal.

FRANK: Well I reckon that was pretty good. I'll make a cook of you yet.

JENNI: But it took forever. It never takes mum more than half an hour to get a meal.

FRANK: Out of a packet and doesn't taste half as good.

JENNI: Lot easier.

FRANK: But not so good for you. Meals like this'll make you big and strong.

JENNI: Sod that. I wannabe a model.

FRANK: Well they don't swear.

JENNI: That's what you think.

FRANK: You can't beat a good stew. Pity I missed the rabbit. That comes of trying to shoot when you're in a temper.

JENNI: You'd put a rabbit in that?

FRANK: Yes.

JENNI: But what about its fur?

FRANK: I told you, you skin and gut it first.

JENNI: You'd not get me doing that.

FRANK: I'd show you how.

JENNI: No way. *She takes the plates to the sink and washes them up.* That's disgusting.

FRANK: Stop moaning. You didn't have to do it. *He takes a book and starts to read. Jenni mooches about the room for a little while, poking about.* Leave my things alone.

JENNI: I ain't doing nothing.

FRANK: You're poking your nose into things that don't concern you.

JENNI: Why ain't you got a tele?

FRANK: I don't want one and if I did I don't suppose I'd get a signal in all these trees.

JENNI: What you do all the time?

FRANK: When I'm not out I read. Sometimes when Sal's here we play Scrabble.

JENNI: Can we do that?

FRANK: It's a word game.

JENNI: We could play Beat Your Neighbour or Newmarket.

FRANK: I don't have any cards.

JENNI: Why not?

FRANK: Because I don't enjoy card games.

JENNI: Why can't I go out?

FRANK: Go if you want but the snow's covered the track and there's more on the way. You'll get lost and freeze to death. You needn't think I'll come looking for you.

JENNI: What a bleedin' hole.

FRANK: Don't swear. It's my hole and I like it. I didn't ask you to share it.

JENNI: You don't care about me do you?

FRANK: Why should I?

JENNI: You're old. Old people are supposed to care about the young.

FRANK: Where did you get hold of that crazy idea?

140

JENNI: Mum said her gran looked after her.

FRANK: Well you are not my granddaughter and your mum was looking after you, but you ran away.

JENNI: She didn't care.

FRANK: So you say.

JENNI: You don't believe me?

FRANK: There's two sides to every story.

JENNI: You don't want me here.

FRANK: What I want is a little peace.

JENNI: What can I do?

FRANK: I don't know. Just shut up, I'm trying to read.

Jenni mooches around and then picks up a screwed ball of paper and unfolds it.

JENNI: Ere, isn't this your letter?

FRANK: What? Oh yes.

JENNI: Don't you want it?

FRANK: No.

JENNI: Why not?

FRANK: None of your business.

JENNI: Didn't Sal think it was special?

FRANK: She can think what she likes, it's none of her business either. It says my home is 'unfit for human habitation' and they're allocating me a flat.

JENNI: What's alli alliwhatsit?

FRANK: Keeping, reserving, putting it aside.

JENNI: For you? A flat? Wow! That's great.

FRANK: There's nothing great about it. What do I want with a box in a box surrounded by other people? I've lived here for fifty years and now they tell me its not fit.

JENNI: Who does?

FRANK: The council. The interfering, nosy, bloody bureaucrats.

JENNI: What's a bureau...?

FRANK: Just shut up will you?

A Pause

JENNI: What did you do here all that time?

FRANK: I was a gamekeeper. I looked after the animals, bred pheasants and partridges. They're birds, big birds, like chickens.

JENNI: What for?

FRANK: For the estate, the family that lived in the big house. They used to have shoots.

JENNI: Shoots?

FRANK: Yes. Parties of half a dozen or more came down to shoot.

JENNI: Shoot the birds?

FRANK: Yes.

JENNI: With guns?

FRANK: Well it wasn't with bows and arrows.

JENNI: That's horrible, cruel.

FRANK: Better than being stuck in a battery all your life.

JENNI: What's a....?

FRANK: For God's sake Jenni! I'm trying to read.

JENNI: Frank?

FRANK: *Sighing.* Yes?

JENNI: D'you still do it? Look after the animals and that, I mean you're ever so old.

FRANK: No. I retired some years ago but I was told I could stay here for the rest of my life and that's what I intend to do.

JENNI: Who told you? The people in the big house?

FRANK: Yes but the estate's been sold, split up and the new owners want me out so they contacted the council.

JENNI: Can't they make you?

FRANK: Over my dead body.

JENNI: You going to top yourself then?

FRANK: Well I hadn't thought of going that far.

Pause

JENNI: I saw someone top themselves.

FRANK: What? When?

JENNI: Last year sometime. February twenty third.

FRANK: What happened?

JENNI: This bloke was standing on the bridge looking into the water. Well on the top bit at the edge.

FRANK: The parapet. And then?

JENNI: Well I didn't think he ought to do that. He was spaced out.

FRANK: What?

JENNI: He was a druggie...he was spaced out. I shouted at 'im; 'Hey mister!' and he jumped. Must have been freezin'

FRANK: Oh my God!

JENNI: I tried to tell a lady but she didn't believe me.

FRANK: Poor chap. *He looks at Jenni who is obviously upset at this memory.* Anything else?

JENNI: I saw him later in the mud. He looked like one of them floppy dolls. Squashed. I don't like seeing dead things.

Frank doesn't know what to say. A silence.

JENNI: Frank?

FRANK: What?

JENNI: What's it about? What you're reading?

FRANK: It's a Dickens. 'David Copperfield'.

JENNI: What's a "dickens"?

FRANK: Who, not what. He's an author, was, he wrote books over a hundred years ago.

JENNI: That book? One hundred years old!

FRANK: Not this one, it's a reprint.

JENNI: Why don't you read something new?

FRANK: Well Dickens was a great writer.

JENNI: What's it about?

FRANK: Well this book is about a boy who runs away after his mother dies, and he's left with his cruel stepfather.

JENNI: Where's he go?

FRANK: To Dover, to an aunt he's never met.

JENNI: What she do?

FRANK: She takes him in and gives him a loving home. He was one of the lucky ones.

JENNI: You said ' this one', there are others?

FRANK: Oh yes. Dickens was a great campaigner.

JENNI: What's a campaigner?

FRANK: A person who fights for a cause. In Dickens' case it was against the exploitation of the young.

JENNI: What's exploiwhatsits?

FRANK: In Dickens' time children as young as six were put to work. I don't mean helping round the house, but working in factories and coal mines.

JENNI: No school?

FRANK: No, but they were poorly paid and worked in harsh conditions sometimes for ten to twelve hours a day. Now I want to read.

He returns to his reading she to her drawing.

JENNI: Frank?

FRANK: What now?

JENNI: Will you teach me to read?

FRANK: No.

JENNI: Why not? You said I ought to learn.

FRANK: I'm not a teacher and it's not something you're going to pick up overnight.

JENNI: I know that, but...

FRANK: The snow's not going to last forever. When the thaw comes we're going to the police and sort you out.

JENNI: I ain't going to no police. You can't make me.

FRANK: Can't I? Just you wait and see.

He returns to his book she opens her mouth to protest but decides on a different tactic.

JENNI: Will you read it to me then?

FRANK: What?

JENNI: About them kids.

FRANK: 'It was a crazy old house abutting on the water when the tide was in, and on the mud when the tide was out, and literally over-run with rats. Its decaying floors and...'

JENNI: I don't want to hear 'bout rats.

FRANK: Well do something else then.

JENNI: What?

FRANK: Why don't you draw? I think there's some paper in the bottom drawer.

Jenni finds some paper and also a photograph, she looks at it and back at Frank, but decides not to say anything and goes back to the table.

JENNI: What'll I draw?

FRANK: Anything.

JENNI: But what?

FRANK: I don't mind. Use your imagination.

JENNI: Have you got any colours?

FRANK: No. Just pencil.

JENNI: You need colours for a proper picture.

FRANK: I haven't got any colours!

Silence. Frank reads, Jenni draws.

JENNI: Who's the photo of?

FRANK: What?

JENNI: The photo, in the drawer. The woman and the baby.

FRANK: What you doing poking about?

JENNI: I wasn't, you told me to get some paper.

FRANK: Why didn't you, instead of being nosy?

JENNI: Who are they?

FRANK: Past history.

JENNI: Is it your mum and you?

FRANK: No.

JENNI: Who then?

FRANK: You ought to be top of the class, all these bloody questions.

JENNI: I only asked who they were.

FRANK: None of your business.

Jenni studies the photograph

JENNI: You bin married?   Is this your wife?

FRANK: Yes!

JENNI: Where is she?

FRANK: Long gone. Now leave it will you?

JENNI: Keep you hair on.   Nice as bleedin' pie ain't you when I'm poking the fire and cooking dinner. *Pause.* What about the baby? You said you hadn't got no children.

FRANK: For Chrissakes! *He gets up and snatches the photograph out of Jenni's hand.* I said leave it! Leave me alone!

Frank storms out into the bedroom. After a moment, Jenni gets up, looks around to see if she could steal anything, then decides simply to leave. She hurries out of the door. After a moment Frank returns and sees that Jenni has left. He goes to the door, opens it and stands looking out as the lights fade...

Act Two Scene 1

The lights come up on the empty room. After a moment or two the door is kicked open and Frank hobbles in half carrying and half dragging Jenni. He takes her across the room and dumps her in the chair.

FRANK: My God girl, you've really done my back in this time. *He goes to put some logs on the fire.* Bugger!

He takes the log basket and hobbles out leaving Jenni shivering uncontrollably.

JENNI: I'm so cold Frank. Frank? Where are you? Don't leave me. *She gets up and goes to the bedroom. She is beginning to panic. She returns and yells.* Frank!!

The door opens and Frank comes in holding an axe.

FRANK: Make yourself useful and put those last logs on the fire and then put the kettle on.

JENNI: Where are you going? Don't leave me.

FRANK: You left me girl. If you remember?

JENNI: Don't go.

FRANK: I've got to get some more logs or we'll both freeze to death. Do some work, it'll warm you up.

Jenni puts a couple of logs in the stove and gets as near as possible to warm herself. Frank re-enters.

FRANK: This should do us. You put the kettle on I see!

He does it.

JENNI: I'm so cold.

FRANK: *Going into bedroom.* 'Course you are you stupid girl. What did you expect? *He re-enters with a jumper, socks and towel.* Take your coat off and put this on. *He hands her the jumper and then, with difficulty, gets down on his knees.* Christ! I don't think I'll ever get up again. *He takes Jenni's shoes and socks off, rubs her feet and puts the socks on again.* What made you do it? You've done my back in.

JENNI: Don't go on about it. I'm freezin',

FRANK: *Hauling himself to his feet. He goes over and pours two mugs of tea into which he puts a large dose of whisky.* You'll get warm. My back's going to be bloody agony for weeks. Here drink this. Don't make a face, you've got to get warm inside as well as out; and get out of my chair. *She does so and he lowers himself into it.* Oh, get me some Aspirin, they're in the drawer by the sink. You could've died, you know that don't you?

JENNI: *Giving him the Aspirin.* I got lost.

FRANK: 'Course you got lost. I'd get lost with the snow covering all the paths. Oh sit down girl and drink your tea. What the hell were you playing at?

JENNI: Well you told me to get out.

FRANK: What?

JENNI: Well you made it clear you didn't want me here.

FRANK: I never said that.

JENNI: You didn't have to. Anyway, Sal was bound to tell the police and they'd come and find me if I stayed. And I never believed you, when you said I couldn't leave. I just thought you wanted me to stay 'cos of your ankle and I felt sorry for you.

FRANK: Well I hope you're a damn sight sorrier now I've done my back in?

JENNI: Yeah.

FRANK: You're wrong you know? About Sal. I'd said you were a niece, and I know she doesn't believe me, but she wouldn't have told the police, or anyone else for that matter.

JENNI: You got a thing going for her have you?

FRANK: What? No. Well once in the dim and distant past maybe. But now, now we're just good friends.   In fact she's the only friend I've got. Not that I mind, suits me fine. *He watches her for a moment or two.* Why are you so frightened?

JENNI: You said you was going to the police.

FRANK: Just so he can get in touch with your mum.   Jim is hardly major crime squad. Have you stolen anything, apart from my coat?

JENNI: No.

FRANK: Drugs?

JENNI: Nothing to get in a sweat about.

FRANK: Look if you're having problems with this man of your Mum's…

JENNI: Dave.

FRANK: Dave, then you've got to talk to someone. If not the police, a teacher maybe.

JENNI: No.

FRANK: Why not?

Pause

JENNI: I might have done for him.

FRANK: Who? Dave? *She nods.* Tell me.

JENNI: He was drunk. I'd just come from the bathroom and hadn't much on, and he made a grab for me, I kicked him in the shins and then pushed him, and he fell backwards down the stairs.

FRANK: Where was your mum?

JENNI: She was at the bottom and was screaming. She'd seen him grab at me and I don't know if she was screaming at me, or him. Anyway he was at the bottom all sort of crumpled and grey looking and his head was bleeding. Mum said I'd killed him and to run. So I put some clothes on and ran.

FRANK: I think we should go to the police and tell them what happened.

JENNI: No.

FRANK: I doubt he's dead anyway.

JENNI: He was ever so still and bleedin'.

FRANK: That doesn't automatically mean death.

JENNI: Well if he ain't dead, he'll beat the living daylights out of me if I go back.

FRANK: Not with your mum there.

154

JENNI: Wouldn't make no difference. He knocks her about an' all.

FRANK: Why't she leave?

JENNI: Don't think I haven't asked her, but he says he's sorry and won't do it again, which is a bleedin' lie.

FRANK: Look if we tell Jim the whole story I'm sure we can get it sorted. Any policeman would be on your side, seeing that you were just protecting yourself, particularly with your mother as a witness.

JENNI: Mum! Don't bank on it. He'll say 'sorry' again and she'll go all soft 'cos she loves him. Him, not me.

FRANK: I'm sure if you'd killed him it would have been on the news.

JENNI: The news? You got a tele?

FRANK: No. Sal told me there'd been a report about a missing girl, nothing about anyone being dead or even injured.

JENNI: Bloody Sal.

FRANK: There's no need for that. You can't just run away and think nobody will care.

JENNI: Is that why you came to look for me?

FRANK: Good riddance, I thought. Now I can get back to my own life without being pestered every five minutes. Only when

155

I went out and felt the wind I knew you wouldn't last, especially as you were going in the wrong direction.

JENNI: How did you know that?

FRANK: You can't walk through the snow without leaving tracks.

JENNI: And you found me.

FRANK: Easily enough. It was getting you back that was a nightmare. Don't see how a little scrap like you can weigh so much. Felt like leaving you more than once, but I'd promised myself, never again.

JENNI: Never again what?

FRANK: Nothing.

JENNI: I wish I had a grandad.

FRANK: I'm sure you have.

JENNI: Don't know where. Mum ran away from her home, her dad used to strap her so I don't want him and she won't talk about my dad.

FRANK: Ah. Well. She probably has her reasons.

JENNI: There's loads of kids at school who parents have split but they get to see their dads.

FRANK: Perhaps he's gone away, abroad even, perhaps he died or...

JENNI: Or perhaps she don't know who it was, but she does 'cos she says he was a bad lot. Don't see how he could be worse than Dave.

FRANK: As I said, she probably has her reasons.

JENNI: Those kids whose dads have left still got grandparents, so she's done me out of them as well, it's not fair.

FRANK: Life isn't.

JENNI: If I had a grandad I could stay with him. *Silence.* When the snow's gone will you show me?

FRANK: Show you what?

JENNI: Where the animals live and where you kept the birds and that.

FRANK: When the snow's gone we're going to sort you out.

JENNI: I'll sort me'self out.

FRANK: How?

JENNI: I'll hitch to Southampton, get a job.

FRANK: No one's going to employ a fourteen year old.

JENNI: I can look older. You thought I was eighteen.

FRANK: No, you said you were eighteen and I didn't believe you.

JENNI: I wannabe a model, they start them young.

FRANK: But you can't read.

JENNI: Don't have to, you just stand in fab clothes looking sexy.

FRANK: There'll be more to it than that.

JENNI: Or p'raps I could get on Pop Idol.

FRANK: What on earth's that?

JENNI: It's on the tele.

FRANK: You're not likely to get on TV.

JENNI: Yes I am. It's for ordinary people who want to be pop stars. They have umm...sort of tests...

FRANK: Auditions.

JENNI: Yeah. There are hundreds of them, and then if the judges like you, you go on to the next round, until there's only two left, and then the people watching votes for who's to win.

FRANK: Can you sing?

JENNI: Better than some of them last time.

FRANK: What happens then?

JENNI: I make loads of money and be like Posh Spice and marry someone like David Beckham. *Frank looks blank.* You don't know who he is do you?

FRANK: Umm...

JENNI: You don't know nothin' do you?

FRANK: Isn't he a footballer?

JENNI: He was only the England captain and he's gorgeous and he's got loads of money.

FRANK: You're chasing dreams girl.

JENNI: Well how are they going to come true if I don't?

FRANK: The likes of you and me can't afford dreams.

JENNI: Some people are lucky.

FRANK: You can't sit around hoping Lady Luck is going to call.

JENNI: There's people who win the lottery.

FRANK: Probably more are struck by lightening. There's a lot of hard work before you can realise your dreams.

JENNI: Didn't you never have no dreams?

FRANK: Well, yes. I would have liked to travel.

JENNI: Why didn't you?

FRANK: You need plenty of money, or be in the travel business.

JENNI: What d'you mean, travel business?

FRANK: A travel agent, a courier, pilot or....

JENNI: An air hostess. I'd like to be one of them. P'raps then I'd meet a millionaire and then I could give you money to travel and your dreams would come true.

FRANK: Thank you. To do any of those things Jenni, you need a good education.

JENNI: Oh don't go on about it. Told you, I can't go home. *Silence.* I didn't know I could kill someone.

FRANK: You didn't, and even if he is dead it was an accident, not like killing someone deliberately.

JENNI: What's it like to kill someone?

FRANK: What? What makes you think I know?

JENNI: You kill birds and animals.

FRANK: That's for food. Not in the same category as killing another human being.

JENNI: I thought...

FRANK: What?

JENNI: You said ' never again'

FRANK: Eh?

JENNI: When you rescued me. I thought p'raps you'd left someone out in the snow.

FRANK: No girl, I've never done that.

JENNI: What then?

FRANK: Nothing. It's all a long time in the past. I'm going to have a tot, do you want another tea?

JENNI: No thanks. Where would you go?

FRANK: What?

JENNI: If you travelled.

FRANK: Here's a book of photographs of some of the places I'd like to see.

Jenni looks through the book, she is not that impressed.

JENNI: It's all mountains, forests and sand.

FRANK: Yes, beautiful wild places.

JENNI: There's nothing to do or see.

FRANK: There are the native birds and animals...you could stand and listen to the silence.

JENNI: Haven't you never travelled then?

FRANK: I've been to Scotland, the Lakes and the like but I've never been abroad.

JENNI: You could go now.

FRANK: It's funny, now you'd need a shoehorn to move me, when I was young I couldn't wait to leave.

JENNI: Why didn't you?

FRANK: God you're a little terrier aren't you? Never let anything go.

JENNI: Yap, yap, yap.

FRANK: I don't really want to talk about it.

JENNI: I told you about Dave.

FRANK: When I was young…

JENNI: A hundred years ago.

FRANK: It seems like it. I was born here. Well, over the other side of the hill. My father was the cowman and my mother worked in the big house. The Graingers owned the estate then. They were O.K, many fared worse than we did, but you had to tip your hat, which I didn't like. I longed to be out of here, but then I was pulled out of school at twelve to work on the farm, and after my National Service I came back as Assistant Gamekeeper .

JENNI: Why did you come back?

FRANK: No money, no qualifications. So I thought I'd come back, save a bit and then go to London, perhaps go to evening classes. I reckoned I had plenty of time, after all I was only twenty. But it didn't work out.

JENNI: Why not?

FRANK: Leave it.

JENNI: How can I? You bang on about education but you did nothin' about it, and then just say leave it.

FRANK: Things happened.

JENNI: What things?

FRANK: I met Betty, she was one of the housemaids. Anyway, I got her in the family way and so we got married and had a son; Peter. And the following year a girl; Jane. *Pause.* On her fourth birthday, we had a so-called party in the woods, just the four of us and the Labrador puppy. It was a beautiful spring day and we had a great time. Such a great time. Betty whinged a bit about the kids getting too excited and overheated but she was a born worrier. Two or three days later Jane caught a chill and the weather had turned. Betty wanted me to take her down to the doctor…

JENNI: Didn't you?

FRANK: No. 'It's late Bet.' I said, 'and cold. She'd be better tucked up warm in bed than me take her out in this cold wind.' I turned in. I had no excuse, except I'd had a long day and a few beers and, as I said, she was a worrier. I slept like a log 'til she woke me in the morning with her screaming.

JENNI: What had happened?

FRANK: Jane was dead. My beautiful, beautiful little girl had gone. Just because I didn't feel like going out. I'd have liked to bury her here, on the hill, the place where she loved to play.

JENNI: Are you allowed to do that? I mean just bury someone, don't they have to be buried in a churchyard or something?

FRANK: Why? What had the church done for us? Betty falling on her knees every Sunday hadn't stopped my daughter from dying. If there is a God, which there isn't. He'd be here amongst the trees and the birds and what better place to lie than where she had had so much joy in her short life?

JENNI: What happened then?

FRANK: Nothing. Why should it? Betty left and I was on my own again, and probably that's how it was meant to be.

JENNI: I don't know how you can stand it.

FRANK: What?

JENNI: Here, all alone.

FRANK: I like the forest.

JENNI: You can't.

FRANK: Why not?

JENNI: It's scary.

FRANK: What's scary?

JENNI: You said animals and birds live there but I didn't hear nothing.

FRANK: That's the snow, deadens all sound.

JENNI: But then I heard the voices.

FRANK: Voices?

JENNI: Whispering. I heard them whispering...about me...and I ran.

She puts her hand out to Frank who takes it.

FRANK: It was just the wind in the trees. It does sound like whispering. I like to imagine it's the trees gossiping, telling their.. *He notices that Jenni has started to cry.* Jenni?

JENNI: I was so cold and so frightened.

Frank pulls her towards him and hugs her.

FRANK: I know girl, I know.

Blackout

Scene 2

The room is empty. Some of Jenni's drawings are on the table. After a moment or two Jenni comes in, she is in Frank's jacket but her trainers and the bottom of her jeans are wet. She goes to the fire to warm herself and is about to take off her trainers when she stops, hurries to the window, looks out and then hurries outside. A moment or two later she returns with an armful of logs, which she puts by the fire. She takes off the jacket, returns to the fire and is just taking off her trainers when Frank comes in. He has his gun but no kill. During the following conversation he puts the gun away, and takes off his jacket and boots.

FRANK: What you been up to?

JENNI: Nothin'.

FRANK: How did you get your feet wet then?

JENNI: Got some logs.

FRANK: There was no need, plenty already in.

JENNI: Well I didn't look. You're always saying 'make yourself useful, get some logs in.' So I did.

FRANK: You usually manage to do it without half drowning yourself.

JENNI: Stepped in a puddle didn't I. Everythin's drippin' out there.

FRANK: Thaw's set in and that, young lady, means we'll go down to the village and see Jim.

JENNI: How we goin'? You're still limping.

FRANK: Use the van of course.

166

JENNI: What van?

FRANK: Don't tell me you haven't seen it? Your nose is into everything.

JENNI: That junk heap out the back?

FRANK: Never judge a bird by its feathers.

JENNI: I've never seen a bird with a ton of rust on its back.

FRANK: It may have a spot of rust but the engine's fine. We'll go down as soon as I get it started.

JENNI: I wanted you to learn me to read.

FRANK: Teach you. I can't.

JENNI: Why not?

FRANK: Told you before, I'm no teacher.

JENNI: There's teachers at school and they ain't done much good.

FRANK: Well you have to want to learn.

JENNI: I do, just told you haven't I?

FRANK: So you can go back to school.

JENNI: But they don't know I can't read.

FRANK: You'll just have to own up, won't you?

JENNI: But if I stayed on a bit and you started me off I wouldn't have to.

FRANK: So it's the teachers' fault now is it?

JENNI: Well no but...

FRANK: No, my mind's made up. You can help by putting the kettle on. I'll just go and turn the engine over.

He exits. Jenni looks after him for a moment and then puts the kettle on, and sits at the table to continue a drawing. There is a knock at the door and Sal walks in.

SAL: Post! Oh, hallo.

JENNI: I thought you weren't coming no more?

SAL: Nice to see you too. I stop at the end of this week. Where's Frank?

JENNI: Out the back trying to get the van started.

SAL: Oh good. I can pop my bike in the back and he can give me a lift to the village.

JENNI: How d'you know he's going to the village?

SAL: Where else would he go? Unless he's going to take you home.

JENNI: Why should he?

SAL: Well you've been here a little while. You want to get home I expect?

JENNI: No.

SAL: I never did quite understand why you came.

JENNI: Told you.

SAL: No you didn't. Frank said there was some upset in the family.

JENNI: That's right.

SAL: What upset?

JENNI: S'not your business.

SAL: No, but it just strikes me as odd you arriving in the middle of the night without any clothes.

JENNI: 'Course I got clothes, wearing them ain't I?

SAL: Without a change of clothes.

JENNI: Who says?

SAL: I haven't seen you wearing anything else and what you have got aren't very suitable, are they?

JENNI: I didn't know it was going to snow.

SAL: Perhaps not but I would have thought...

JENNI: There wasn't room O.K? My gran's ill, and all the family are down, and there's no room. O.K?

SAL: I'm sorry to hear that.

JENNI: Reckon she's going to die.

SAL: I'm sorry.

JENNI: Don't really know her.

SAL: Oh. Well. What are you drawing?

JENNI: Nothing.

SAL: Hardly nothing. I do admire what some people can convey with a few strokes of a pencil. You must have an excellent art teacher.

JENNI: No one taught me. I just do it.

SAL: That's amazing but they're very violent aren't they?

Jenni shrugs and carries on drawing for a moment or two.

JENNI: Is Frank's wife dead?

SAL: I shouldn't think so.

JENNI: Don't you know her then?

SAL: I did, when she lived here.

JENNI: Where she live now

SAL: I haven't the faintest idea.   She upped and left after..a long time ago.

JENNI: Why?

SAL: That's not my business, or yours.

JENNI: If you're such an old friend I thought you'd know.

SAL: Why? After all I didn't even know he had a brother.

Jenni scowls at her and returns to her drawing.

SAL: Well I'm going to make some tea. I expect Frank would like a cup after working out in the cold. What about you?

JENNI: No thanks.

SAL: *Going to the store cupboard for the tea.* Goodness. No wonder you're going to the village you seem to be reduced to baked beans and tea bags.

JENNI: I like beans.

SAL: Well just make sure he buys something sensible. I hate him living out of tins. I wish he'd move.

JENNI: Where to?

SAL: They're building some retirement flats in the village. I mean, being isolated like this when you're his age is just silly and pig headed.

JENNI: Why's he live here all alone?

SAL: You'd better ask him yourself.

JENNI: I have and he said he liked it.

SAL: Well then.

JENNI: But he ain't got no radio or tele or even a 'phone.

SAL: I know. He's not very fond of people.

JENNI: He likes you, and I think he likes me.

SAL: He must do.

JENNI: We're people.

SAL: We are individuals. I don't think he regards us as part of the general public.

JENNI: But why don't he like them?

SAL: Something happened, a long time ago.

JENNI: He told me about Jane.

SAL: Did he now? Well Betty blamed him, as if he didn't blame himself. But she told everyone, even Peter. I mean the boy was only five and he was trotting around and saying 'my Daddy killed Jane.' Then she left. One day she was here and then she was gone. I gather there was an enormous row. Everyone turned against him.

JENNI: But you were his friend.

SAL: Not then. I was the post-woman so I did see him. The man was a wreck, but one day I managed to...

JENNI: What?

SAL: Nothing. All water under the bridge now, best forgotten. Goodness the poor man must be frozen out there. *She makes the tea and goes to the door and calls out.* Tea up! Would you like one?

Jenni shakes her head. Sal pours out two mugs. Frank enters.

FRANK: What you doing here?

SAL: What a welcome I've had from you both. Anyway you're becoming popular there's another letter for you.

FRANK: I thought you'd given up.

SAL: I retire at the end of the week. Did you get the van started?

FRANK: Yes.

SAL: Good you can give me a lift down.

FRANK: O.K.

SAL: That Salisbury woman was on the news again this morning asking her daughter to come home. Apparently there was a row and the girl ran away the night before the snowstorm.

Frank drinks his tea not looking at Jenni who is concentrating on her drawing. She's especially worried because the girl hasn't any warm clothing.

FRANK: Why are you telling me this?

SAL: Just thought you'd be interested.

FRANK: Well I'm not. Finished? *He takes her mug and puts them both in the sink.* You ready?

SAL: Oh for goodness sake, let's stop this charade.

FRANK: What charade?

SAL: You know that I know Lizzie is not the granddaughter of a non-existent brother. She's Jennifer Spencer, the runaway.

FRANK: Spencer. I knew Smith was a lie.

JENNI: Frank!

SAL: She's got to go home, either voluntarily or we tell the police.

JENNI: No!

FRANK: She's got problems.

SAL: So have you, she can't stay here.

FRANK: I know. She knows, I've told her.

SAL: Then we need to go to the Police.

JENNI: I won't go to the Police! You can't make me!

Jenni exits to bedroom.

FRANK: Look, she will go, but she's got to do it in her own time.

SAL: OK. But this can't go on forever...

FRANK: I know.

Jenni re-enters,

FRANK: Look, Sal and me are going to the village, but I promise we won't do anything, won't see the police or call your mother...

SAL: Poor woman...

FRANK: That poor woman hasn't been great shakes as a mother to date so she can suffer a little longer.

SAL: I hope we're doing the right thing...

FRANK: We don't do anything, nothing at all without talking to her first. O.K.?

SAL: OK.

JENNI: You promise?

SAL: I promise.

FRANK: Right let's go. A couple of bottles are top of the list.

SAL: *To Jenni.* Will you be all right on your own?

FRANK: You're not going to run away again are you?

JENNI: No.

Frank and Sally exit and Jenni watches them from the window.

Blackout

Scene 3

Later the same day. Jenni and Frank are sitting eating fish fingers. The letter Sally delivered earlier is lying on the table between them.

JENNI: You ain't read your letter.

FRANK: I know what it's about.

JENNI: What? Oh it's about that flat.

FRANK: Yes.

JENNI: Why don't you want the flat? I mean you'd have the tele and electric light...

FRANK: I've got electricity.

JENNI: That works; and street lights and buses and.....

FRANK: You and I young lady will never understand one another and that's a fact. You're listing all the things I don't want. I've lived here fifty years. Oh it could be more comfortable but I go out early and see the deer and sometimes at night I gaze at the stars and the silence is, what d'you say? It's cool.

JENNI: But what if you're ill?

FRANK: I'm ill now, someone's done my back in.

JENNI: I mean really ill, dying.

FRANK: I'm quite happy to die here, but not yet. No the thing that gets me most is that I was promised, promised and that goes for nothing. Never make a promise you can't or won't keep.

JENNI: I've seen on the tele when people won't move they come with bulldozers and dig holes and knock the houses down.

FRANK: Well I'll have to put up the barricades won't I?

JENNI: Can I help you?

FRANK: No.

JENNI: You can't put up barricade with a bad back.

FRANK: I reckon I'll get a few more threatening letters before they send in the bulldozers. *He opens the letter.* The buggers!

JENNI: Who?

FRANK: The bloody council. They say they're going to evict me next month.

JENNI: You going to build them barricades?

FRANK: Not yet. But I won't take it lying down. Sod them!

He screws the letter up and throws it away.

JENNI: Won't you need that?

FRANK: You're right. Not just a pretty face are you?

JENNI: Have you finished with your plate?

FRANK: Yes thanks, you know, those fish fingers weren't bad.

JENNI: Ain't you had them before?

FRANK: No. Sal said you'd like them.

JENNI: Oh.

JENNI: If Sal makes me go to the police, I'll tell them what I've seen.

FRANK: I don't know what you're talking about.

JENNI: When I was lost I saw the graves.

FRANK: Graves?

JENNI: On the hill. I'll tell them about the graves where you've buried Jane, and probably Betty and Peter as well.

FRANK: *Laughs.* I'll give you ten out of ten for imagination. Jane was cremated and Betty took the ashes with her when she went back to her family in Scotland with Peter. I never heard from her again and I don't know if she's alive or dead. I must admit I've felt like killing her more than once, but its difficult to commit murder if you don't know where to find your victim.

JENNI: But what about them graves?

FRANK: Dogs. If you could read the markers you'd see their names. Silky, a Springer Spaniel; Murphy, a black Labrador; Caesar, a brown Labrador; and Buster, mixed parentage. Each one much loved.

JENNI: I didn't think you buried dogs.

FRANK: Why not? They were all good friends and deserved better than be tossed on a bonfire or be turned into cat food. So I'm afraid you can't blackmail me.

JENNI: But you promised.

FRANK: I only promised we wouldn't go to the police when we went down to the village, but Sal's right, at the very least we've got to contact your mother.

JENNI: But then she'll know where I am, unless you took me away.

FRANK: I can't do that.

JENNI: You're all talk ain't you? You say you care but you don't, you just want to get rid of me.

179

FRANK: No that's not true, far from it. But taking you away is not the answer.

JENNI: It'd be O.K. if I said it was. I was thinking about it. We're near the sea ain't we?

FRANK: Well its not too far away.

JENNI: Well you and I could go down and live in a boat on the beach like Peggotty and you could look after me.

FRANK: I don't know that I'd fancy living in a boat but I'm afraid if the council don't like the idea of someone living in a little house in the wood, they certainly wouldn't want them on the beach.

JENNI: But we could go to a quiet bit where they wouldn't know.

FRANK: There's not going to be any boats or cottages. You cannot live with me.

JENNI: I'd go to school. Every day.

FRANK: That's got nothing to do with it.

JENNI: You don't want me.

FRANK: What I want doesn't come into it. It just wouldn't be allowed. I'm not a relation. People would just think I was a dirty old man and, in the end, the authorities would force you to leave.

JENNI: That's not fair. Not if I wanted to stay. And you wanted me to.

FRANK: It doesn't work like that. Until you're old enough, your family or the social services are responsible for your well being.

JENNI: What? I might go into care? But in David Copperfield he...

FRANK: That's just a story. And anyway the world's changed a lot since then. Not all of it for the better I admit but we are more caring of our children.

JENNI: I'm not going back.

FRANK: You're worried about Dave aren't you? Look, he will be dealt with.

JENNI: Will he go to prison?

FRANK: If you testified I should think it highly likely.

JENNI: I'd like that, but I don't want to go into care.

FRANK: Think about it. It wouldn't be forever.

JENNI: No! I'm not doin' that!

FRANK: If you don't go with Sal, what else are you going to do?
JENNI: I don't want to go with her.

FRANK: Sal's got your wellbeing at heart.

JENNI: Your wellbeing.

FRANK: Whatever.

JENNI: Well I'll leave. It's what I was going to do in the first place. I'll go to Southampton and get a job.

FRANK: Just think about it girl. Even if I gave you a few quid the money would soon run out. No one is going to give you a decent job. You're not stupid, you know what'll happen. You'll end up on the streets and someone'll get you on to drugs. You've seen druggies, you know what their life can be like. You walk out of here I won't see you again.

JENNI: You're threatening, just 'cos I won't do what you want.

FRANK: No. But I won't know where you are and you won't be able to let me know.

JENNI: I'd get someone to learn, teach me, to write.

FRANK: Why should they? An uneducated girl would be much easier to manage. If you go with Sal, you'll get an education, maybe even catch one of your dreams.

JENNI: Do you think I could be an air hostess?

FRANK: I don't see why not, then you'll be travelling, living my dream as well.

JENNI: You'd write to me?

FRANK: Of course, but only if you promised to write back. It's your choice. Either way I'll get my bed back.

JENNI: If I go, you and her'll tell the police and they'll pick me up.

FRANK: We'd have to sooner or later.

JENNI: Not much of a bleedin' choice is it then? And you said I could trust you.

She goes into the bedroom and slams the door.

Blackout

Scene 4

The room is empty for a moment, and then Jenni comes in wiping sleep from her eyes.

JENNI: Morning Frank. Frank? *She goes to the window and looks out.* Bloody hell! *She gets down the pot from the dresser where she found the money before.* Mean old bugger.

Frank enters.

FRANK: Good morning Jenni, you're late up. Looking for money?

JENNI: No. It's empty anyway.

FRANK: I thought it better not to leave temptation in the way.

JENNI: I thought you liked me.

FRANK: My liking's got nothing to do with your sticky fingers. No one's trained you yet.

JENNI: What d'you mean?

FRANK: I can like a puppy but I won't leave it in a room with a plate of food before I've taught it not to steal.

JENNI: I ain't no puppy dog.

FRANK: Children and puppies are just the same. Mischievous, inquisitive, disobedient. And loveable. Sal's here.

JENNI: I saw. Can't get rid of me quick enough, can you?

FRANK: She'll wait until you're ready.

JENNI: Going to have a long wait then.

FRANK: Come on girl, don't make it hard.

JENNI: I thought you liked me?

FRANK: I do. I do. Very much.

JENNI: But not as much as your precious postie.

FRANK: It's not a competition.

JENNI: If it weren't for her, I could stay.

FRANK: If it weren't for her, there wouldn't be any place for you to stay.

JENNI: What d'you mean?

184

FRANK: You asked me if I was going to top myself if the council turned me out. I wouldn't dream of doing such a thing, but a long time ago, Sal stopped me doing just that.

JENNI: You were going to kill yourself?

FRANK: She walked in, bright and breezy the day I was seriously considering blowing my brains out.

JENNI: Bloody hell! Why?

FRANK: A lot of things had been said to me and about me, and I just didn't think much of the world in general. Sal. Well she persuaded me it wasn't all bad, and she'll tell you the same.

JENNI: If she was so bleedin' marvellous why didn't you marry her?

FRANK: She was already married and she was very fond of her husband.

Sally enters quietly. Jenni is unaware of her.

JENNI: So she's bleedin' Wonder Woman but if I don't go with her she's going straight to the police.

SAL: No. Frank has made me promise. If you go we'll forget you were ever here, as if we never knew you existed.

JENNI: You wouldn't forget me Frank, would you?

FRANK: No, but if we can't keep in touch the memory might fade.

JENNI: *Pause.* O.K. *Turns to Sal.* I'll go with you. Ready?

SAL: Have you got your things?

JENNI: I didn't have nothin'

FRANK: Here. *He fetches his coat and we see him put some notes in the pocket.* It's still cold out. *He helps her into it.* Go to school now, I want you to write to me.

JENNI: *Crying.* You'll write back?

FRANK: Always.

SAL: Come on then.

Jenni nods, turns and runs out the door. Sal follows her. Frank goes to the window and raises his hand in farewell. Sighing, he turns back into the room. He goes to the stove and bends to put on a log when his back gives way. He gives a cry of pain.

FRANK: Arrgh! Give us a hand girl. *Remembering, he struggles to the table and slowly straightens himself.* Oh Jenni. *As he looks round the room Jenni returns.*

JENNI: Frank?

FRANK: Yes?

JENNI: I just…I thought perhaps you might borrow, lend me, that Copperfield book…?

FRANK: Of course, you can have it. It's on the chair.

186

JENNI: *As she picks up the book.* You alright?

FRANK: I'm fine. I'm fine. Give it here a moment.

She passes it to him and he writes in it and gives it back to her.

JENNI: *Looking at the inscription.* What's it say?

FRANK: *Looking over Jenni's shoulder, he reads.* 'To my little terrier, the best of the lot' *Jenni turns and gives Frank a big hug.* Right. Get along with you now, Sal's waiting. *Just as she is leaving Frank calls out.* Oh and Jenni, perhaps you could tell Sal she can show me round those new flats tomorrow?

JENNY: Right.

She leaves and as Frank looks round at his home.

Blackout

At the Hop
by
Shiona Morton

First performance: 15th September 2005 West Tytherly Hall, Hants.

Characters and doubling : (original cast and production team)

Edie – Ruth Curtis
Vivien/Mum/Child – Rebecca Hulbert
Jimmy/Alf – Edward Jaspers
George/Dad – Matt Pinches
Stage Manager – Dominic Phillips
Designer – David Haworth
Director – Sean Aita
Literary Manager/Dramaturg – Nell Leyshon

This play was originally written as a co-commission with Farnham Maltings.

Edie's memory 1: Childhood

Hopping song. Actors come on stage singing and beating a rhythm with the hop poles and setting them up in rows on stage.

They say that 'opping's lousy
We know that it ain't true
We like to go a 'opping
To earn a quid or two
Wiv an eh ih oh
Wiv an eh ih oh
Wiv an eh ih eh ih oh.

EDIE: At the end of August the East End left London and took the train to the 'op fields. Our street had been getting ready all summer, cleanin' the 'oppin' pots, collectin' this 'n that, puttin' aside tins and stores. The cupboards were burstin' with all their treasures. But my family was different. Our treasures were in heaven.

Store your treasures in the bank of heaven
Where no thief can steal away
There you'll find them safely waiting for you
When you get to heaven - one day!

EDIE: We were temperance. We were chapel. We 'ad nothin' to do with the demon drink. So no 'op- pickin' for us. My friends got excited about goin' away to the country on the train and missin' school for a whole month but I knew I'd be stayin' put.

CHILD: Edie, Edie, we got our letter!

EDIE: Did ya?

CHILD: We got the number of our basket.

EDIE: What number are ya?

CHILDREN: We're five, we're five, we're always number five.
We're always number five.

EDIE: When the letters came I knew they'd soon be off.

Actors' voices take a line each with this rhyme.

Tea chests packed with 'opping pots / Primus stove and welly
boots / Borrow a barrow from Mr Finn / Pile it high, we'll get
it in.

EDIE: The street would be empty 'cept for a few dads stayin' in
London to work.

Dad'll push to London Bridge / Don't go near The Rising Sun /
Once he's in he won't come out / We'll miss that train without a
doubt.

MAN: Ta now! See yer at the weekend. Pick plenty of 'ops and
bring 'ome some money wiv yer. Think of Christmas!

WOMAN: Ta, our dad, keep outa that pub!

EDIE: And they were gone. Four long weeks of quiet streets
and empty classrooms. Four weeks of waitin' for all their
stories of hoppin' huts and campfires and pickin' into brollies
and playin' in the alleys. I knew all about it and I'd never been.

CHILD: Brought ya someink Edie, a present!

EDIE: Ave ya?

CHILD: Don't tell your dad, he won't like it.

EDIE: What is it?

CHILD: A handful of 'ops. Smell 'em.

EDIE: So I did. Bitter and sweet. I'd smelt it before, wafting in the air outside the brewery. When we passed there my mum would grab my 'and and rush me on. Den of iniquity she said. I wondered what iniquity was like. Now I had a handful of it. Hops. I wrapped 'em in a hanky and hid 'em. They were my secret.

Song again, softly.

The hops they are a-waiting
They grow upon the vine
We'll get there nice and early
And shout to "pull the bine"
Wiv an eh ih oh
Wiv an eh ih oh
Wiv an eh ih eh ih oh

EDIE: Then one year something 'appened.

DAD: I've been called.

MUM: What?

DAD: I've been called by the Lord.

MUM: Oh my word. What's he called you to do?

DAD: I 'ave been called to save sinners, so we must go where the sinners are.

MUM: Not Africa! Please tell me we are not goin' to Africa!

DAD: The chapel is empty but the hop fields are full and ripe for the Lord's harvest.

EDIE: I couldn't believe my ears. I was goin', I was goin' at last.

DAD: Let us pray.

Edie's prayer whispered over Dad's (Marked with / to show separation)

May God bless our going out. May the sinners hear his word
May they turn from wicked deeds/ Thank you God for callin'
Dad/ May we sow eternal seeds/ I'm glad that it's not Africa but
Kent and hops and all the rest!/

We go amongst the heathen now/ I promise I will do my best/
We know they need your saving grace. Provide for us oh Lord
we pray/ I will be good, I will not pick / As we preach your
word today / I'll sing and pray and speak for thee/ Your word
may fall on rocky ground / I'll never ever touch a drop/
The soil be poor or scorched by sun / Just see and smell the
bitter hops/ The travail long and hard may be. Our harvest Lord
is souls for thee.

EDIE: So in 1922 we joined the Mission to Hop Pickers. When everyone packed we packed. When they pushed their barrows to the station we pushed ours.

It's time to go a hopping
It is that time of year
We laugh as we get ready
We'll soon be out of here

Sounds of a train station.

VOICES: All aboard! All aboard! / London Bridge to Avenhurst / Close the doors! Close the doors!

Whistle and sound of train leaving.

Busy crowded London Bridge / Barrows, tea-chests everywhere / Kids are lost and found again / Hoppers all on platform ten.

EDIE: Our mission family board the train. We almost look the same as them. And though I know it isn't true, I pretend I'm going hopping too.

Scene One

Sunday Morning 1957. Church bells and the sound of rock 'n roll on the radio. Jimmy is outside Vivien's house. Vivien is in her dressing gown putting on lipstick.

JIMMY: Viv! Vivien! Come down 'ere!

VIVIEN: Jimmy! What are you doing 'ere? Quiet. No one's up.

JIMMY: Come on, we're goin' out.

VIVIEN: I got work later

JIMMY: It's Sunday.

VIVIEN: It's a favour, for Mr. Marsh.

JIMMY: Well you can tell old Marshy he can forget it. You're comin' with me.

VIVIEN: I can't. I promised.

JIMMY: We're goin' out. All of us. We're leavin' at ten. Three cars. Now get your stuff.

VIVIEN: I told you Jimmy.

JIMMY: And I'm telling you, so do it.

VIVIEN: I don't like it when you speak to me like that.

JIMMY: So? You're my girl and you do what I say.

VIVIEN: Not if I'm not your girl.

JIMMY: You fancy old Marshy do ya?

VIVIEN: No.

JIMMY: You met another bloke?

VIVIEN: No.

JIMMY: Good, 'cos if you 'ad, I'd kick his 'ead in. Remember that. I wouldn't be too 'appy with you neither. You understand?

VIVIEN: You can't go round thumpin' people all the time.

JIMMY: Is that right? Oh go to work if you like. I'll pick you up later and we'll go for a little spin all on our own.

VIVIEN: Jimmy. I don't want....

JIMMY: Course you do! See you later darlin'

He kisses her and goes. She sighs and watched him leave. Rock 'n roll music is louder then melts into George singing the same song as he comes in on a pair of stilts.

EDIE: George, Georgie! You're 'ere. I've been lookin' all over.

GEORGE: Boss wants this finished.

EDIE: Why? What's the 'urry? You get down from there.

GEORGE: He's payin' extra mum. I'm goin' to finish it.

EDIE: You are not. I've laid out your suit and tie. If you don't 'urry up we'll be late.

GEORGE: I'm not comin' mum.

EDIE: Get down from there so I can talk to you proper. Georgie! Get down from those stilts!

GEORGE: You should 'ave a go mum. You can see the 'ole valley from up 'ere.

EDIE: I'd never get up on those things and neither should you.

GEORGE: Better than prayin' inside any day. It's beautiful this mornin'. I could get used to being twelve foot tall. King of the hop fields. King of the countryside!

EDIE: You're not listenin' to me.

GEORGE: I told you mum, I'm not comin' to church.

EDIE: George, just do somethin' nice for your old mum.

GEORGE: I can't. We've got a meeting with Marsh this morning. There's goin' to be changes. Big changes.

EDIE: What big changes? Stop wobblin' on them things. You're doin' it on purpose to worry me.

GEORGE: I could dance on these mum. I could dance and turn a somersault and not come off.

EDIE: Tell me.

GEORGE: You won't like it.

EDIE: All the more reason.

GEORGE: Marsh is sellin' 'op pickin' machines. Next summer it'll all be mechanised.

EDIE: Machines? 'Ow can they pick 'ops with machines?

GEORGE: Tractor tears down the bines. This new machine of Marsh's strips off the 'ops.

198

EDIE: No pickers?

GEORGE: Just a driver and a few girls as checkers. That's it.

EDIE: But that's terrible.

GEORGE: I said you wouldn't like it.

EDIE: You got to stop 'im.

GEORGE: Me?

EDIE: Next summer?

GEORGE: He wants them as soon as possible. Sooner he gets 'em, sooner he makes big money. He's gonna be a rich man our boss.

EDIE: But there'll be no more hoppin' not like it was.

GEORGE: You got to move with the times, mum. Nothin's like what it was.

Edie's memory 2: Six to Sixteen

EDIE: When you're a child time's different.

CHILDREN: Come on Edie. Hide and seek. I'm on it, 1,2,3,4,5,6,7,8,9,10. Comin' ready or not!

EDIE: The Lord kept callin' my dad year after year. While he saved sinners I played in the 'op gardens.

Edie creeps down the alley.

ALF: I see ya!

EDIE: Alf!

She runs up and down and is caught by Alf.

ALF: Saw ya! Saw ya miles off!

EDIE: I gotta go now. My dad wants me to sing.

ALF: Come and pick with us tomorrow.

EDIE: I can't. I'm not allowed.

ALF: I won't tell.

EDIE: The others might.

ALF: No they won't. I won't let 'em. Come on Edie. Pickin's the best.

EDIE: A'right.

EDIE: They all kept my secret. Alf helped me clean the black resin off my fingers so's I could get back to the meetings just in time.

Edie races into place and stands up obediently with others.

One two three the devil's after me
Four five six he's always throwing sticks
Seven eight nine he misses every time
Hallelujah hallelujah amen.
Nine eight seven I'm on my way to heaven

Six five four he's knocking at the door
Three two one the devil's on the run
Hallelujah hallelujah amen.

EDIE: Years went by. I began to grow up and so did my playmates. It was harder and harder to keep my secrets.

ALF: Hello Edie.

EDIE: Hello Alf.

ALF: Just got 'ere?

EDIE: Just off the train.

ALF: You look different.

EDIE: Do I?

ALF: All grown up.

EDIE: I'm sixteen next week.

ALF: Sixteen.

DAD: Edie, help your mother on the wagon please.

EDIE: Yes Dad.

ALF: 'Ere I'll do that. You get on the wagon with your mum. You're a lady now.

DAD: So Alf, 'ave you given your heart to the Lord yet?

ALF: Can't say I 'ave sir.

DAD: Time you did my lad. I'll share a verse or two with you as we ride along. Today could be the day the Word of God speaks to your heart.

ALF: You all right there ladies?

Alf winks at Edie and she smiles.

MUM: Edie, he's a nice boy, but he's not saved.

ALF: Off we go then.

EDIE: And the two big shire 'orses started and the wagon trundled 'eavy with sinners. Everything smelt green. London was dirty in them days. Fog and filth. You prickled with dirt. When I got on that wagon I felt like the coal man, like someone who wanted a wash. Course it was 'ot. We'd left early when it was chilly so we'd peel off our things, till our mucky skin got baked. As we trotted out of the station my dad started savin' souls.

DAD: Let me share this text with you. John chapter three...

EDIE: I marked each place as we passed, same as last year, same as last year: the village clock, the colours in the hedgerow, the trees that grew in a clump....

DAD: Should not perish, but have everlasting life.

EDIE: All here. All still here.

ALF: Look there it is! There it is Edie!

EDIE: And he turned and looked right at me. The kids stood up and nearly toppled the wagon.

ALF: Sit down you lot!

MUM: Sit down Edie. You're a big girl now.

EDIE: He was still lookin'. I felt my cheeks burn. Then everyone shouted as we came closer and saw the hop gardens with their tall green tunnels ready for pickin', and our farm, our farm, waitin' for us once again.

Scene Two.

The farm kitchen 1957. Vivien is sitting smoking a cigarette. George comes in.

GEORGE: Afternoon.

VIVIEN: God! You nearly gave me 'eart attack! *Stubs out cigarette.* I thought you were Mr. Marsh. He hates smoking.

GEORGE: You'll be in the doghouse will ya?

VIVIEN: Well he's got to watch his step, askin' me to work Sunday.

GEORGE: You work for 'im?
VIVIEN: Yeah. I'm his secretary, well his general dogsbody. I run around after 'im. He likes that.

GEORGE: I bet he does. I hope he's payin' you plenty.

VIVIEN: Why do you think I'm doing it? I told him, I said Mr Marsh, this is my day off. If you want me to drive you all over the country you 'ave to make it worth my while.

GEORGE: And what did he say to that?

VIVIEN: What could he say? He needs a driver so he 'ad to put his 'and in his pocket and dig out a ten shillin' note.

GEORGE: I see. Not bad!

VIVIEN: He can afford it. It wasn't easy gettin' away neither I can tell you.

GEORGE: Why's that then?

VIVIEN: None of your business.

GEORGE: Ooh! Sorry for asking!

VIVIEN: Some people can't take no for an answer that's all. What's your name?

GEORGE: George.

VIVIEN: I'm Vivien, as in Vivien Leigh. Only I'm not Leigh, just the Vivien. My mum called me after 'er. Thinks she's beautiful, which she is, and a film star of course which I would like to be in one way, but not in another, if you know what I mean. Anyway now she's off 'er trolley in't she? Or they think she is. They're tryin' to cover it up but I read in a magazine that she was "showing signs of a nervous collapse" whatever that is. Sounds bad. Do you know what that is?

George shakes his head.

GEORGE: Not really.

VIVIEN: Me neither. I think she's just plain crazy, out of 'er 'ead. So let's hope that I don't end up like her eh? Even though she's my namesake an' that. I'd like her money though.

GEORGE: You talk a lot don't ya?

VIVIEN: Yeah, it gets me into trouble. Keep puttin' my foot in it. My mum's always tellin' me, she says Vivien watch yer mouth! And she's right. Think first speak after.

GEORGE: Good advice.

VIVIEN: But I never remember. I try, but before I know it, I've said somethin' I shouldn't. George....d' you work here?

GEORGE: What would I be doin' in this kitchen if I didn't work on the farm?

VIVIEN: I'm in this kitchen.

GEORGE: I was going to ask you about that when I got a word in edgeways.

VIVIEN: I was sent in 'ere by Mr. Marsh and your boss to make tea which, as you see, I haven't done. I thought I'd 'ave a quiet fag then you turned up and put me off.

GEORGE: Oh it's my fault is it?

VIVIEN: Well I've 'ad to introduce myself, it's only manners! And I don't know where anythin' is! It's just as well you're 'ere 'cos I reckon Marshy boy'll be gettin' twitchy for 'is tea. I dunno. I type, I drive his car, I make his tea. Might as well be his mother.

GEORGE: I don't think that's what he's got in mind.

VIVIEN: Don't you start!

GEORGE: What?

VIVIEN: Nothin'.

GEORGE: Dunno what you're complainin' about. That's a very nice car.

VIVIEN: So?

GEORGE: He lets you drive it!

VIVIEN: Only 'cos he can't.

GEORGE: You're jokin'!

VIVIEN: I'm not. I'm sworn to secrecy. He's tried often enough but he's failed his test over and over again. He pretends that he has a "chauffeur" as he calls it, 'cos he's posh, but he can't do without me really.

GEORGE: I can see that.

VIVIEN: He likes a girl driving him, for obvious reasons. To be honest, I don't think there's a lot goin' on there. Someone with a bald patch as big as 'is needs a bit of glamour in his life.

GEORGE: And you're the glamour?

VIVIEN: So he thinks. I do try. Course no one knows about the test but me and he'd hit the roof if anyone found out so don't say a word or I'll lose my job. Mind you maybe that wouldn't be so bad. I've just noticed George, you're really short.

GEORGE: You're quick off the mark.

VIVIEN: Come over 'ere. You're only up to my nose. How did that 'appen?

GEORGE: I 'ad an accident.

VIVIEN: No! What on the farm?

GEORGE: Yeah. Dreadful it was. Fell under a tractor. Chopped me legs off.

VIVIEN: George, that's horrible!

GEORGE: I know. Sliced me poor old legs in two. They couldn't save the middle portion but they were able to sew the ends back on so I got me feet back. You can't even see the join.

VIVIEN: You're 'avin me on aren't ya?

GEORGE: You asked so I told you.

He is laughing now.

VIVIEN: Very funny!

GEORGE: You don't believe me?

VIVIEN: You're a rascal George. You 'ad me feelin' sorry for you for a minute. Not that you deserve it.

GEORGE: Oh I do really. I'm just a little lad.

VIVIEN: I'll need to watch you.

GEORGE: Good I'll enjoy that.

VIVIEN: Cheeky! Now tell me the truth. Why are you short, really?

GEORGE: Just didn't grow. Least my legs didn't.

VIVIEN: Don't you start gettin' rude.

GEORGE: Me? Nothin' is further from my mind.

VIVIEN: You're not bad lookin' apart from, you know, being short. You got lovely eyes.

GEORGE: You're not bad lookin' yourself, apart from you know, bein' loud. You got lovely legs.

VIVIEN: Oh!

They laugh.

VIVIEN: I like you George. You don't mind do you? About my big mouth?

GEORGE: No I don't mind.

VIVIEN: Told you I always said the wrong thing.

GEORGE: Not all the time.

Pause. They look at each other and then away.

VIVIEN: You'd better go in. They're waitin' for you to choose a machine. They reckon you'll know what's what. How come you know so much?

GEORGE: I'm the hop expert.

VIVIEN: Big 'head.

GEORGE: It's true. Born and bred 'oppin' I was.

VIVIEN: I come here 'oppin' once.

GEORGE: Did ya? I don't remember you.

VIVIEN: It was years ago, when I was tiny.

GEORGE: That's why! You couldn't speak then.

VIVIEN: Very funny. There were 'undreds of kids.

GEORGE: Won't be next year. It's all change. No more hand pickin'.

VIVIEN: Course. Marshy's machines. Oh that's sad in it? I remember it was great fun. Like campin'. Well it was for a kid.

GEORGE: You should come again. Come for the last one. Before we get the machines. It'll never be the same again.

VIVIEN: You're gettin' all soppy George. Why should I come and pick 'ops?

GEORGE: Lots of reasons.

VIVIEN: Like?

GEORGE: Like I'll be here for start.

VIVIEN: Yeah and?

GEORGE: Oh I thought that might do it.

VIVIEN: Sure of yourself in't ya? Go on, tell me why I should come to your last hopping. It's got to be good.

GEORGE: OK. Because you'll see the 'op gardens first thing in the mornin' before the sun burns off the mist. Because you'll learn all the songs and you'll always know 'em and you'll remember the sound of people singin' in the field on a sunny day. Because you'll smell the 'ops dryin' in the kiln, and you'll cook on a fire, and when you're old you'll be able to say you were there for the last pickin' and you'll know somethin' no one else will know.

Pause.

VIVIEN: Oh George.

GEORGE: What?

VIVIEN: You and your words. Very good. Very good I must say. You 'ave a way with words. Do you know, I might just come 'oppin'. I might just take you up on that. You're a bit of a surprise George, in't ya?

Edie's memory 3: Forbidden Fruit

Alf pulling Edie by the hand in the hop garden.

EDIE: Alf, Alf I can't. You'll get me into trouble. I can't just run off and pretend I'm playin'.

ALF: Why not?

EDIE: 'Cos I'm growin' up.

ALF: I can see that.

EDIE: And they want me to help with the meetings.

ALF: Do you want to?

EDIE: It's not up to me. I don't want to upset them.

ALF: Why should they get upset?

EDIE: You know they think it's wrong.

ALF: There's nothing wrong with what we do Edie. It's just 'ops. 'Ere, these are for you. *Gives her a bunch of hops.* Should be a flower really but I like these better. Smell 'em.Picked 'em right off the top. Best in my alley, in the whole 'op garden.

He tries to kiss her.

EDIE: Alf...you can't do that.

ALF: It's your birthday. Sweet sixteen and never...

EDIE: How do you know?

ALF: Oh. I've got competition have I?

EDIE: No. But you'll have to catch me first.

ALF: All right. Ready?

EDIE: Ready. Bet you can't catch me.

ALF: Bet I can.

She runs off. He chases her. Her mum calls.

MUM: Edie! Edie!

Alf catches her and kisses her as Mum walks in.

MUM: Edie, what are you doing? *They jump apart.* Come 'ere. Come away from that boy.

EDIE: Mum, it's Alf.

MUM: I know who it is. Off you go Alf and leave 'er alone.

Alf goes.

EDIE: Mum!

MUM: What do you think you're doin? Runnin' after boys.

EDIE: He was runnin' after me.

MUM: Watch your lip. He's not saved. You don't know what he might do.

EDIE: Alf would never do me any 'arm.

MUM: So you say. Remember Edie, you might be in the world but you're not of it. You must separate yourself from sin.

EDIE: They made me do a lot of prayin'.

DAD: Lord bless the soul of your daughter Edith. Keep her from temptations of this sinful world in which we live. Save her from backsliding.

EDIE: I loved my dad. I loved to watch him pray.

DAD: Bring her once more into the safety of your flock. Help her to keep separate from the world and its godlessness.

EDIE: He stood up and spoke to God, liftin' his face and his 'ands, bouncin' a little on his shinin' shoes.

DAD: Save her from the depths of waywardness and the path to destruction.

EDIE: Light on his closed eyes. Heaven in his 'eart, glory in his soul.

DAD: We pray this in the name of our Lord and saviour...

EDIE: But all I could think of was the shower of raindrops and pollen when a bine fell down, and the smell of 'ops and wood smoke on a hot afternoon, and the singin' echoin' round the garden, all the people hymnin' hoppin' songs as they filled their bins together. And Alf's arms around me, holdin' me tight, willin' me to hold him back, and his kiss, soft and sweet on my lips. All of it, all of it, forbidden fruit.

Scene Three

1957. Loud rock 'n roll music. George is singing along to his transistor, doing up his tie and practising his moves to the music. Edie comes in with the tally box and starts looking through cards and lists.

EDIE: Can't you leave that thing upstairs?

GEORGE: The whole point about the 'thing' mum is that you can take it anywhere.

EDIE: I wish you'd take it away. I can't hear myself think. I don't know how much that thing cost but whatever it was, it was a waste of good money.

GEORGE: Thirty guineas of good money.

EDIE: What? No George!

GEORGE: That's how much it was.

EDIE: But that's a fortune. Where did you get that kind of money?

GEORGE: I saved. Where else? I've earned it.

EDIE: You can't spend thirty guineas on a wireless.

214

GEORGE: It's not a wireless mum, it's a transistor radio fresh from the US of A. They're the latest thing. Hardly anyone's got one.

EDIE: I'm not surprised at that price. How could you waste your money like that?

GEORGE: It's not a waste. You wait. One day, I'll look back and say George; you were one of the first blokes in the whole of England to own a transistor radio.

EDIE: Thirty guineas.

GEORGE: It's my money.

EDIE: You could 'ave 'ad a lovely new suit, two with that.

GEORGE: Mum, I give you my wages every week. I haven't kept you short. This is my overtime.

EDIE: Sunday work.

GEORGE: Some of it.

EDIE: You didn't tell me how much it was.

GEORGE: Do I 'ave to?

EDIE: In my day....what came in, a family shared .

GEORGE: What are you sayin'? You want my overtime as well?

EDIE: No.

GEORGE: Well then. If I earn it and you don't need it, I reckon I can spend it.

EDIE: You used to tell me everythin'. It's just you and me. We've got to look after each other. Put that thing off!

GEORGE: I'm goin' out now.

EDIE: Where you goin'?

GEORGE: Town.

EDIE: Who are you goin' with?

GEORGE: People.

EDIE: Who?

GEORGE: People I know.

EDIE: There's been trouble at these dances.

GEORGE: I can look after myself.

EDIE: And what would happen if someone started on you?

GEORGE: I'd start on them.

EDIE: Oh yeah, big talk, but you couldn't Georgie.

GEORGE: Here we go again.

EDIE: Before you go, you can give me a hand.

GEORGE: No I can't. I'll be late.

EDIE: It'll only take a minute.

GEORGE: Why 'ave you got the tally box out?

EDIE: You always liked the tallybox didn't you? When you were little you'd take everythin' out and play with it.

GEORGE: Mum...

EDIE: All my treasures are in 'ere. Things I 'ad from when I was small. I've kept everythin', not just tallies. I got all the names of the 'oppers, all the baskets and 'uts . Lists and lists of 'em.

GEORGE: Well you won't be needin' them much longer.

EDIE: Come and read 'em out while I do the letters.

GEORGE: You're jokin'!

EDIE: No, it'll take me half the time.

GEORGE: Mum, I'm goin' out.

EDIE: We can sit and 'ave a cup of tea and a chat while we're doin' it. You can even keep your wireless on if you turn it down.

George turns off his transistor and picks it up. He hesitates and then walks out.

GEORGE: Don't wait up mum.

Edie's memory 4: Proposal

EDIE: I went down to Kent every year with the mission. My mum and dad lived in 'ope that I'd find myself a nice chapel boy and I wasn't short of offers! But every 'opping I saw Alf and every year I was more sure.

Hymn at open-air service. Edie, Mum and Dad singing. Alf watching.

When he cometh when he cometh to take up his jewels
All his jewels precious jewels his loved and his own
Like the stars of the morning his bright cloud adorning
They shall shine in their beauty bright gems for his crown

Dad begins his sermon.

DAD: When he cometh....when he cometh. Where will you be? Will you be ready? Today many of you have toiled for your harvest of hops. Some of you will have been slack. But when the whistle blew, what then? The tallyman came to measure your harvest did he not? Whether you toiled or slacked, the Tallyman came. I tell you today my friends, the Tallyman cometh. Our work will always be measured. There is always a tally, a price to be paid, a cost to be counted. God is the great Tallyman. He will come and he will measure us for eternity. Are you ready to answer to him? How many bushels of faith? How much will you have to show? When God, the Tallyman cometh, will you be ready?

Repeat hymn.

Alf gestures to Edie. She sneaks away with Alf to the hop kiln. Edie takes a breath in.

218

ALF: What is it?

EDIE: It's the autumn. I can smell it. Smelt it this morning when I got up.

ALF: Cheer up. I got potatoes to roast.

EDIE: Have you?

ALF: Yeah it's a feast for you Edie. Cider and hot potatoes cooked in the kiln. What more can a girl want?

EDIE: Nothin'. Cider and potatoes will do me.

ALF: Don't have too much now. It'll go to your head.

EDIE: I got an excuse. I'm goin' home tomorrow.

ALF: Yeah. I was thinkin' about that.

EDIE: I'm tryin' not to.

ALF: I'll come and see you at Christmas like last year.

EDIE: And I'll be back next summer. You'll write letters won't you Alf?

ALF: Course I will

EDIE: And I'll write back.

ALF: Edie?

EDIE: Yeah?

ALF: How would it be if this time you stayed?

EDIE: I can't stay. I got a job back in London.

ALF: You could have a job here.

EDIE: Not much call for a factory girl on a farm.

ALF: No I mean you could do a different job.

EDIE: And what would that be?

ALF: Well I don't know, but if you were my wife I'd work your fingers to the bone.

EDIE: Your wife?

ALF: I don't want you to go back Edie, not this time, not again. Stay here and marry me. Well will you?

EDIE: What do you think?

Scene Four.

1957. Rock 'n roll dance music. Jimmy and Vivien are dancing. Jimmy begins to show off and dances by himself, leaving Vivien looking embarrassed. At first they are shouting over the music.

VIVIEN: Let's go outside!

JIMMY: You wanted to dance!

VIVIEN: Not on my own!

220

JIMMY: Can't stand the competition eh?

VIVIEN: I want to talk to you.

JIMMY: It's like that is it? I don't blame you Viv, I'm irresistible. We can talk in my car.

VIVIEN: I just want to talk. I'm serious.

They go outside. Music fainter. Jimmy starts kissing Vivien.

VIVIEN: Stop it Jimmy!

JIMMY: What's wrong?

VIVIEN: Just stop it!

JIMMY: You wanted to go outside.

VIVIEN: Not for that.

JIMMY: What for then?

VIVIEN: Jimmy, I don't want to go to Brighton on holiday.

JIMMY: I got it all booked. I always go to Brighton. I like it. You've only been once.

VIVIEN: Once is enough.

JIMMY: All my mates'll be there.

VIVIEN: I want a different holiday.

JIMMY: You want too much.

VIVIEN: No I don't.

JIMMY: It's all sorted and you're comin'.

VIVIEN: I got ideas of my own you know.

JIMMY: Course you 'ave darlin'. Mine are just better that's all. Oh my God! You don't want to get engaged do you? Is that it? Just 'cos your friend's got a ring on her finger. You want one do ya?

VIVIEN: No I certainly do not.

JIMMY: Why? What's wrong with me?

VIVIEN: Jimmy, getting engaged usually means you're gonna get married.

JIMMY: Yeah, well we will. One day.

VIVIEN: Will we?

JIMMY: Don't you want to marry me?

VIVIEN: You don't want to marry me!

JIMMY: Well not right now.

VIVIEN: I want to go hop-pickin'.

JIMMY: *Laughing.* Hop pickin'?

VIVIEN: I mean it. In August. I'm goin' to take a few weeks off or maybe even leave my job. I'm fed up with it.

JIMMY: You want to spend your holiday with filthy Londoners and gyppos when I can take you away in my car? Forget it. Come on let's go inside and have a dance.

VIVIEN: No I'm stayin' here.

JIMMY: Look I told ya. I start things, I finish things. If you go off, I'll find ya and I'll bring you back. Get it? Suit yourself. I'll see you in there, and don't be too long, I don't like sulky birds.

Jimmy exits. Vivien looks annoyed. Lights a cigarette. George enters.

GEORGE: Well, it's the lovely Vivien!

VIVIEN: Hello George.

GEORGE: You all right?

VIVIEN: Yeah, yeah I'm fine.

GEORGE: You seem a bit quiet, compared to the other day.

VIVIEN: Do I?

GEORGE: Definitely. My ears are still ringin' .

VIVIEN: Well they ain't heard nothin' yet..'cos I am mad!

GEORGE: Not with me I hope.

VIVIEN: Some people get on my wick. They won't listen. No matter how many times you tell 'em. No matter how many different ways you try to say it. They just don't get it. Cos they don't want to get it. They don't want anythin' to change. They want everythin' to go on the way it always has year in year out and it can't can it? 'Cos people change. You don't feel the same way as last year. You don't want the same things as last year. Do you know what I mean George?

GEORGE: Oh yeah. I know someone just like that.

VIVIEN: Do ya? So do I.

GEORGE: Still, That's better.

VIVIEN: Sorry?

GEORGE: You. Sounded more like your old self.

VIVIEN: You takin' the mick again?

GEORGE: One minute you're as quiet as a mouse. The next, you can't stop the flow. A raging river you are.

VIVIEN: D'ye know, I reckon you're a bit of a poet George. That's your true...what's the word?

GEORGE: Vocation.

VIVIEN: That's it. Like nuns. You should write a book.

GEORGE: Well I might one day.

VIVIEN: You could sell it and make a fortune.

GEORGE: Sounds good to me. I wouldn't mind livin' a life of leisure.

VIVIEN: Not me. I get bored. If there's one thing I hate it's sittin' around havin' nothin' to do.

GEORGE: Oh I don't mean doin' nothin'. I mean doin' all the things you've always wanted to do, but couldn't because you were busy doin' all the things you 'ad to do.

VIVIEN: What 'ave you always wanted to do?

GEORGE: Learn to fly a plane.

VIVIEN: You're jokin'.

GEORGE: No, I've always wanted to fly, ever since I was a lad.

VIVIEN: You could've gone in the RAF. Done your National Service. They'd 'ave taught ya.

GEORGE: Too short. Dodgy leg. Believe me, if they'd taken me I'd 'ave gone.

VIVIEN: Pity. You'd 'ave looked nice in the uniform.

GEORGE: Wouldn't I ! Still nothin' I can do about it. I just 'ave to take lessons, buy a plane, fly a few 'undred hours then I'll fly you wherever you like milady. Where do you fancy? France? Monte Carlo? America?

VIVIEN: Monte Carlo please. Sounds very glam. Suits me you see.

GEORGE: It does indeed and because you look so fantastic this evenin' your wish is my command.

VIVIEN: You are a nutter George.

GEORGE: No I'm not. I mean it.

VIVIEN: I know one thing.

GEORGE: What's that?

VIVIEN: I don't wanna be in this place the rest of my life.

GEORGE: Me neither, but then, I won't be.

VIVIEN: No, you'll be whizzin' about up in the sky.

GEORGE: 'Ere, let's go in and 'ave a dance.

VIVIEN: I can't.

GEORGE: Why not? I like this record.

VIVIEN: I came out for a breather. It's a bit 'ot in there.

GEORGE: You don't want to dance with me.

VIVIEN: Yes I do.

GEORGE: I'm too short aren't I?

VIVIEN: Is that what you think? Come on then, let's dance. 'Ere give me your 'and.

GEORGE: We can't dance out 'ere.

VIVIEN: Why not? The music's loud enough.

GEORGE: If anyone sees us they'll think we're mad.

VIVIEN: Well they'd be right, wouldn't they?

They dance. Jimmy enters.

JIMMY: So we've stopped sulkin' 'ave we?

George and Vivien stop dancing and move away from each other.

VIVIEN: Hello Jimmy. This is Ge....

JIMMY: I don't care who he is. What are you doin'?

VIVIEN: Dancin'.

JIMMY: I can see that. Well you must be desperate to dance with little Tich here.

VIVIEN: Jimmy...

GEORGE: Leave it Vivien.

JIMMY: Yeah you do that. You go and find another dwarf to dance with. You'll be able to reach her arms then.

VIVIEN: Jimmy! Please.

JIMMY: Am I embarrassin' you? You stay away from her mate or you'll be sorry.

Edie's memory 5: Marriage

EDIE: A girl grows up dreamin' of her wedding day. A summer mornin', proud parents and pink roses.

DAD: Be ye not unequally yoked together with unbelievers.

EDIE: Dad...

MUM: For what fellowship hath righteousness with unrighteousness

DAD: And what communion hath light with darkness?

EDIE: Dad, listen please....

MUM: What part hath he

DAD: That believeth with an infidel?

EDIE: Alf is not an infidel! He just sees God in a different way.

MUM: There is only one way Edie. You know that.

EDIE: No, no I don't think I do.

DAD: Wherefore come out from among them and be ye separate saith the Lord.

EDIE: I don't want to be separate. I love him.

DAD: This union is not of God.

EDIE: How can you say that? Alf and me are meant to be together. We always 'ave been ever since we was kids.

DAD: If you choose this path, you turn your back on God, and you turn your back on this family.

EDIE: What do you mean?

DAD: We choose to be separate from the world. We cannot follow you down the road to sin.

EDIE: But I want you to marry us. *No reply.* You will come to my wedding? Mum? You can't just shut me out. I'm your daughter. I'll always be that, won't I?

Mum and Dad turn away.

Wedding March

EDIE: That September Alf and I got married in a little country church surrounded by hop fields. It was the end of the summer. At least I had pink roses.

GUESTS: To Alf and Edie! / Edie and Alf! / Speech, come on Alfred, a speech!

ALF: On behalf of my wife and I *(cheers),* I would like to thank everyone for comin' today and making this such a happy occasion. Edie and I met on this farm and we hope that we will 'ave many 'appy years together. Well...drink up everyone and 'ave a dance!

Music. Everyone dances. Other actors dance offstage leaving Edie and Alf alone.

ALF: Cheer up Edie. This is meant to be the happiest day of your life.

EDIE: It is Alf. I am happy.

ALF: But you wish they'd come.

EDIE: They could 'ave sent somethin'. They could 'ave wished us well.

ALF: No point in gettin' upset.

EDIE: I'm not upset. I'm angry.

ALF: You're mine now. It's you and me that matters. Our family.

EDIE: If I ever have a daughter....

ALF: You will. We will. Girls and Boys. Lot's of 'em.

EDIE: I will love 'em and I will never let 'em go.

ALF: See this hop garden. Looks empty dun it? But before you know it we'll be plantin' and stringin' and startin' all over again. Be the same for us Edie.

EDIE: Will it?

ALF: Course. We've got all our lives ahead of us here. We'll make a family you and me. You can put the past behind you. We're goin' to be 'appy.

EDIE: But my anger didn't go away. I couldn't forget. The plantin' and the stringin' came and the pickin' came round again, but no sign of a baby.

ALF: Stop broodin' It'll 'appen when it 'appens.

EDIE: God the Tallyman. Maybe my dad was right. There's always a tally, a price to be paid. He preached that the day you asked me to marry you.

ALF: You sayin' you were wrong to marry me?

EDIE: No!

ALF: Because that's nonsense Edie, superstitious nonsense. If anythin' was meant it's you and me, do you hear?

EDIE: Yes.

ALF: You're my wife now and you got to put these doubts away.

EDIE: I don't 'ave doubts.

ALF: Dun't sound like it to me. Forget what your dad said. What's ungodly about this life? The farm, the 'ops, good honest work in God's earth. A sup of cider and a man who loves you. What can be wrong with that?

EDIE: I never mentioned it to Alf again. I kept quiet. I buried my bitterness. In time a baby was on its way. Alf was so happy there was a littl'un comin at last. But I worried, and when Georgie was born.

DOCTOR: There's a malformation. Nothing serious. The right leg is abnormal. He'll always limp and he may not grow to full height, but otherwise you have a bouncing baby boy.

EDIE: I knew then that my dad had been right. My life with Alf had a price and my little boy would have to pay it.

Scene Five.

The farm. 1957. Edie crosses the stage with buckets, brush, cloths. Vivien comes on. She is agitated, stops Edie.

VIVIEN: Hello. Is George about?

EDIE: George?

VIVIEN: Yeah he works here. Small bloke. Quite good looking though. Nice eyes.

EDIE: I know who he is.

VIVIEN: Do you know where can I find him?

EDIE: He's workin'.

VIVIEN: So am I. It'll only take a few minutes.

EDIE: We're very busy. Hopping starts today.

VIVIEN: That's why I want to talk to him.

EDIE: You say you're workin'?

VIVIEN: I brought some stuff from Mr. Marsh.

EDIE: I thought that was Marsh's car.

VIVIEN: He'll be gettin' me a lorry if he thinks it's cheaper. He's so tight you wouldn't believe it. He still owes me for last week. Do you know....

EDIE: The deliveries go in the yard.

VIVIEN: I know. *Pause.* I can wait if he's really busy. Or go and find him.

EDIE: Who?

VIVIEN: George. He's the one I came to see. Well I'll go and 'ave a look round.

EDIE: Our boss doesn't like strangers wanderin' around the farm.

VIVIEN: I'm not a stranger love. I've been 'ere many a time sorting out his orders. When you get your nice new shiny pickin' machines it'll all be down to me.

EDIE: Really?

VIVIEN: Oh yeah. Without me nothin' gets done. Marshy's accounts are goin' to be in chaos. Still that's his problem. I'm finished.

EDIE: You're leavin' your job?

VIVIEN: I am. I've 'ad enough of Marshy and his bald patch. I mean he's got a nice car but he is so boring! All I do is type, type, type all day long. I'm turnin' into a typewriter. I need a change and quick. Need to get away. It'll be nice to come 'ere and stay for a while. When you're 'ere you feel you're miles away from town. It's another world. No one will 'ave a clue where I am will they?

EDIE: You wanna come pickin' 'ere?

VIVIEN: Course. Reckon George can get me a job?

EDIE: It's not up to George.

VIVIEN: But he'll help me. He's a nice bloke and once I explain.
EDIE: Explain what?

VIVIEN: Oh. Just that I need a change. Quick. Need to get away. He'll understand. And he's the one that said I should come. He said it was my last chance, you know before the machines.

EDIE: Well you'll know all about that.

VIVIEN: Look can you give him a message? I'll come back this afternoon once I've given Marshy my news.

EDIE: What's the message?

VIVIEN: Could you just say Vivien says sorry about the dance and could she take him up on his offer? He'll know what I mean. Thanks. I'll be back later. Bye!

Vivien walks off and Edie stares after her unsmiling.

Edie's memory 6: Flying

Sound of wartime planes roaring through the sky. It is 1940 people are working in the hop-garden, singing.

Run rabbit run rabbit run run run
Don't give the farmer his fun fun fun
He'll get by without his rabbit pie
So run rabbit run rabbit run run run.

Run Adolf, run Adolf run run run
Why not give Tommy his fun fun fun
We'll get by without your Jerry lies
So run Adolf run Adolf run run run

EDIE: When the war came we kept goin'. Our little boy grew, though not as much as he should. I watched 'im like a hawk. One by one all the young lads went from the village. At least Alf was a reserved occupation. Thank God he was safe.

WOMAN: Did you hear somethin'? SSsshhh stop singin'.

EDIE: I like singin'. It keeps me going.

WOMAN: No listen. I heard somethin'. Could be a plane.

They stop and listen.

EDIE: Georgie, Georgie come here. Where are you? Come 'ere!

ALF: He's all right Edie. What's the matter?

WOMAN: A plane. I thought I heard a plane.

EDIE: I hear it. I hear it now.

ALF: Right everyone down! Come on! Everyone on the ground quick! Georgie over here beside us. Yeah, look, I can see 'em. There they are. Down everyone on the ground!

WOMAN: Might be all right. Might just be headin' home.

ALF: Depends whose they are. Here they come!

GEORGE: It's a Jerry dad, it's a Jerry plane.

ALF: Get your 'ead down. Under me. Come on.

Sound of planes roaring and stuttering over the hop garden. People scream.

GEORGE: They've got 'im. They've got 'im dad. Look!

EDIE: Something was fallin' in flames not far from us, and then there he was in the sky, a figure floating down free as a bird.

ALF: He's comin' down on the farm!

EDIE: Suddenly everyone was up, runnin' as fast as their legs could carry them. I couldn't move.

236

GEORGE: Come on mum, it's a Jerry!

EDIE: George, you come here! But he was off with his dad. They weren't scared, they were excited. You could see it in Alf's face, in the way he held his breath. I ran after everyone else. I wanted to see. When I got there a crowd stood round the parachute and in the middle lookin' scared, with blood on his face was a lad. He couldn't have been more than nineteen. Alf spoke to him.

ALF: You come with us. You come.

EDIE: The boy nodded. Alf smiled a little. As the men walked him off to the farm, in the distance I saw the smoke from his plane, risin' to the sky in a line like a burnt offering.

Repeat verse of the song

EDIE: Don't worry.
ALF: It's all very well you saying don't worry. That boy was half my age. Everyone's lookin' at me thinkin' he's not in uniform, why not? He's not old. What's wrong with him?

EDIE: They're not Alf. Honest, they're not.

ALF: Mrs Huntley in the shop lost her lad. He was at school with me, two years below. I couldn't look at her to say sorry.

EDIE: You're a reserved occupation. Everyone knows that.

ALF: I'm the youngest man still 'ere. Ploughin' up the top field, diggin' for victory. It's not the same is it? No chance I'll get shot or sink or lose a leg.

EDIE: What you do is important. You know that. People need food. They need farmers.

ALF: I should be fightin' like a man. I shouldn't be hidin' 'ere behind a woman's apron strings.

EDIE: You're not hidin'. You're supposed to be 'ere.

ALF: Who says Edie? Who says?

EDIE: I do. You're needed. You know that. I need you. I couldn't stand it Alf if anythin' 'appened to you.

ALF: The other women manage.

EDIE: You're not a coward Alf.

ALF: No I'm not. And I'll prove it.

EDIE: You think you'll be like that boy in his plane? What if he hadn't got out? He'd 'ave burned in there Alf, burned to death and only a lad. What's the point of that?

ALF: I'm goin' into town. I'll see you later.

Alf walks out.

EDIE: He walked out. He'd never done that before. Never left on a harsh word. When he walked back in that evening he handed me some papers. He'd volunteered for the Air Corps.

238

Scene Six.

1957. The farm.

VIVIEN: George! I wondered where you were.

GEORGE: Hello.

VIVIEN: I left a message this morning. I've 'anded in my notice. I'm comin' hoppin'.

GEORGE: Really?

VIVIEN: Yeah. I said I might.

GEORGE: That's not what I remember.

VIVIEN: I'm sorry. I should've come to see you. Apologised.

GEORGE: What do you see in him anyway?

VIVIEN: He didn't used to be so bad. I've tried to get out of it but he just doesn't listen. He's started turnin' up in the mornin' and walkin' me to work. He says he finishes things, not me.

GEORGE: So you're scared of him?

VIVIEN: He waits outside, keeps followin' me.

GEORGE: Does he know you're 'ere?

VIVIEN: No. We're supposed to be goin' to Brighton.

GEORGE: When?

VIVIEN: Today. *George raises eyes and sighs.* I got nervous. I needed to get away from him. It's drivin' me mad. Then I thought of you and your hoppin'.

GEORGE: What as a last resort?

VIVIEN: No! Aren't you pleased to see me?

GEORGE: You'd better keep your 'ead down. It won't take 'im long to find out where you are.

VIVIEN: Maybe I should go. If he comes 'ere he'll cause trouble.

GEORGE: And if you go back it starts all over again dun it?

Edie comes in carrying the tallybox, tucking a list back inside.

EDIE: George! I've done the huts. Put everyone where they were last year.

GEORGE: Mum, this is Vivien. Vivien, my mum, Edie.

VIVIEN: Mum?

EDIE: We've met.

GEORGE: Oh. When?

VIVIEN: This mornin'. I left the message with your mum.

GEORGE: You didn't tell me.

EDIE: I've been busy all day. Haven't 'ad a minute to speak to anyone. You need to collect the pickers at five. They'll be at the station. You best get in that lorry.

GEORGE: Vivien's comin' hoppin'.

EDIE: Really? I don't know where we'll put 'er. We're full up you know.

VIVIEN: I don't mind roughin' it. Honest. I'll squeeze in with some other girls.

EDIE: I don't think there's a place. We've got lots of pickers this year.

VIVIEN: It's my last chance. Last hoppin' you said.

EDIE: That's right. Your machines put paid to that.

GEORGE: I don't think that's Vivien's fault, Mum.

EDIE: She said...

VIVIEN: I told your mum I'd done all the orders. Well, if there's no room.

GEORGE: It's all right. You can have mine.

EDIE: George?

VIVIEN: What?

GEORGE: Why not? I'll sleep in the kiln. I love it in there.

EDIE: You won't 'ave a decent bed for a month.

GEORGE: Who will? It's straw and tickin' for everyone. I'll be fine. I always wanted to sleep there when I was a kid but you'd never let me. It'll be a dream come true.

VIVIEN: Not another one! Him and his dreams. Him and his flyin'!

GEORGE: Vivien, I'll take you to your room.

EDIE: Flyin'?

GEORGE: It's this way.

VIVIEN: Yeah. Planes, you know. He must 'ave told you that one! Mad isn't he? Still, I quite fancy Monte Carlo and you did say you'd fly me there George?

GEORGE: That's right, I did.

VIVIEN: What's wrong?

GEORGE: Look mum...

VIVIEN: Have I said the wrong thing?

Edie's memory 7: Fire

EDIE: When Alf went away I did the tally. I marked the cards, called out the basket numbers, weighed the 'ops. I put everything in a cake tin with my lists and cards and numbers. Georgie used to like to play with it when he was little. He was the one who called it the tallybox.

WOMAN: You done them books?

EDIE: Hope I got 'em right. *Packing cards in the box.*

WOMAN: Course you did. Alf would be proud of you. Let me see. Nice photo. He's a handsome fella Edie.

EDIE: He is isn't he?

WOMAN: Come on. No news is good news.

EDIE: Did you hear them planes last night?

WOMAN: Bad night on the coast.

EDIE: I can't sleep thinkin' of him up in one of them things day after day.

WOMAN: Alf's as stubborn as a mule. He won't let anyone shoot him down, you'll see.

EDIE: No one's safe, are they?

WOMAN: It will be over soon. The war can't last forever.

Sound of planes. Edie holds the box as if it is her baby until the end of this speech.

GEORGE: Mum! Mum!

EDIE: I woke up. I knew somethin' was wrong. Then I heard it, a tiny buzzin' then louder and louder. It was an engine failin'. I wasn't thinkin' about the pilot. I was movin', runnin' for my son in the dark. I was runnin' but I felt I was walkin' through mud. I didn't think I'd get to my boy on time. That Jerry was so loud above us as he flicked the switch and dropped his last two bombs. And then the explosions came, great boomin' sounds and the house shook, and the ground kept shakin' and we fell down, me and Georgie, and he screamed and screamed. When we looked outside, the top field and the village were burnin'.

Scene Seven

1957. Edie's cottage. Edie still holding the tallybox. Sound of car door slamming. Jimmy enters, dressed up and smoking a cigarette.

JIMMY: Hello there. I wonder. Could you by any chance be Edie?

EDIE: Who are you?

JIMMY: Jimmy. Pleased to meet you. Have I got it right? You are Edie?

EDIE: Who told you that?

JIMMY: I asked at the farm. It's a lovely name. Sorry to bother you Edie but I'm looking for my girlfriend.

244

EDIE: She's a picker is she?

JIMMY: No she's not.

EDIE: Well how would I know her?

JIMMY: Someone said you'd talked to her.

EDIE: I've been talkin' to people all day.

JIMMY: Oh very clever Edie, very clever. 'Ere, what's in that tin? You're holdin' on to it tight. Got some cash in there have you?

EDIE: No.

JIMMY: Oh I bet you 'ave Edie. I know what you ladies are like. You hide it all under your mattress don't you? Got 'undreds stashed away in there I expect. Let's 'ave a look.

EDIE: Really it's just a box of ...

Jimmy pulls it away from her and turns away.

EDIE: Give me that back!

JIMMY: Oh. Got a temper 'ave we Edie? I'm just 'avin a little gander at your tin. that's all. You'll get it back. As long as you tell me what I want to know.

EDIE: Give it back please.

JIMMY: What's in 'ere then? Oh, lots of little cards with numbers on. They're not in any order are they? What if I just scattered them 'ere? Would that make any difference?

EDIE: Don't do that! Please!

JIMMY: Oh, sorry. Slipped out of my hand. We'll pick 'em up in a minute shall we? When you've told me where my girlfriend is.

EDIE: I don't know your girlfriend.

JIMMY: That's not what I've heard. You know Edie today we're goin' on holiday. It's a special occasion. I've got the car all packed and I've got my glad rags on. Did you notice I'm all dressed up? Did you? Did you notice my jacket? What do you think? Go on, say somethin'. I won't be offended.

EDIE: Very...very modern.

JIMMY: It is isn't it? Jimmy Dean had one just like it. You go to the pictures Edie?

EDIE: No.

JIMMY: You should. You should. I'll come and take you out one evening. How about it? We'll go up the Beaumont next Sunday and see Rebel. It's brilliant. I've seen it twenty, thirty times. Gets better and better. You'd love it.

EDIE: I don't go out on a Sunday.

JIMMY: You're the holy type are you Edie? Because if you're the holy type I know that you're telling the truth when you say that you haven't seen my Vivien.

EDIE: Vivien? She's your girlfriend?

JIMMY: Yeah. We're thinkin' of gettin' engaged. Actually I thought I might pop the question while we were away. What do you think?

EDIE: I don't know.

JIMMY: We could buy a nice ring in Brighton couldn't we? You got one in 'ere Edie? Let's see.

EDIE: Don't empty it out please.

JIMMY: Oh look a photo. Who's this? This your bloke Edie? He's a handsome chappie! See, I know you girls like a bit of romance. I know what you're like. Flowers, down on bended knee. That what he did? Your bloke? Romantic was he, in his day? Wouldn't like anythin' to happen to such a nice piccy. *He holds the cigarette up to the picture.* You seen her Edie?

EDIE: I have seen a Vivien.

JIMMY: Aahh! I thought so. And she's comin' back is she?

EDIE: I suppose so.

JIMMY: She with your boy?

EDIE: What?

JIMMY: Your son. George isn't it? *Holds up baby picture and laughs. Circles it with the cigarette.*

EDIE: How do you know George?

JIMMY: Oh we've met George and me. Just the once. Thing is Edie I think Vivien feels a bit sorry for old George. You know what I mean? He's on the small side isn't he? And he limps along hippity hop, hippity hop. I wouldn't like him to get any silly ideas. I mean Vivien's quite a girl, quite a looker. He's not in her league and just because she's bein' friendly he might think poor lad, that she's got other intentions, which she hasn't because she is about to get engaged to me. You see don't ya?

EDIE: Yes, I see.

JIMMY: So if you'll just tell me where they are.

EDIE: They've gone to the station to collect the pickers. In the lorry. They won't be back for hours.

JIMMY: Thank you Edie. Good girl!

EDIE: Can I have my box now please?

GEORGE: *Off.* Mum!

JIMMY: Oh I think I'll 'ang on to it for a minute. Just in case. I know how much it means to you.

George and Vivien enter.

JIMMY: Hello Viv, George.

248

GEORGE: What are you doing here?

JIMMY: I've come to collect Vivien.

GEORGE: You all right Mum?

JIMMY: Edie's fine. She's been very helpful. She didn't realise we were goin' to Brighton Viv.

VIVIEN: I'm not going to Brighton.

JIMMY: Course you are. It's all booked up, has been for months. Why would you want to stay in this dump?

EDIE: Don't you dare...

JIMMY: Edie love, shut up and stay out of this.

GEORGE: Don't speak to my mother like that.

JIMMY: What are you going to do about it short-arse?

VIVIEN: Jimmy!

EDIE: Nothin'. Just go away both of you. We don't want any trouble.

GEORGE: If Vivien doesn't want to go she doesn't have to. She can stay here if she likes.

JIMMY: I don't think so.

VIVIEN: I am not going to Brighton. I've told you Jimmy, again and again. I don't know what you're doin' here.

JIMMY: I'm here because I don't give up easy and because Shorty here is taking a liberty.

VIVIEN: Stop it.

JIMMY: And if he doesn't keep quiet he's going to get a bloody nose.

GEORGE: Vivien, do you want to go to Brighton?

VIVIEN: No.

GEORGE: Then you're welcome to stay.

Jimmy thumps George. Edie screams.

VIVIEN: Stop it Jimmy. This is ridiculous.

George gets up and thumps Jimmy. They fight. Jimmy gets a hold of George.

VIVIEN: Jimmy is this how you think you can change my mind? Why would I go with you? Just go away and leave me alone.

JIMMY: You want him rather than me? Look at him. He can't walk straight. He's three quarter size. I was going to buy you a ring in Brighton, I was.

VIVIEN: I don't want a ring. You don't get it do you Jimmy? You just don't get it.

Jimmy throws George down.

JIMMY: Well you stay with your midget but don't think it's finished. I finish things Vivien. I always finish things.

Jimmy throws the contents of Edie's box all over the floor and goes off. She runs to pick up the contents. Vivien goes over to help her. George gets up and looks after Jimmy.

VIVIEN: I'm so sorry Edie. It's all my fault. I'm sorry about your things.

EDIE: He was goin' to burn 'em.

GEORGE: What?

EDIE: He put his cigarette right up against your dad's picture.

George moves to pick up the cards.

GEORGE: We'll pick 'em up.

VIVIEN: Yeah, we'll sort it all out.

EDIE: Leave it. Leave it. I think he's goin' to do somethin' else.

GEORGE: What do you mean?

EDIE: I just got a feelin'.

VIVIEN: What could he do? It's me he's mad at.

GEORGE: You mean somethin' at the farm?

EDIE: There's all those pickers Georgie - and kids.

GEORGE: Right, I'll go up there. We might 'ave to get the police.

VIVIEN: I'll come with you.

EDIE: Vivien.

VIVIEN: Yes Edie?

EDIE: You be careful.

As Edie picks up the items from the tallybox, Vivien and George move forward and face the audience. Smoke fills the stage. Edie holds the tallybox the way she did during the bombing scene. Her lines reflect that memory.

GEORGE: Can you smell burning?

VIVIEN: I can see it. Look. Smoke. Over there.

EDIE: I knew somethin' was wrong.

GEORGE: It's the huts.

VIVIEN: What?

GEORGE: The huts, the hoppin' huts. They're filled with straw.

EDIE: First a tiny buzzin' then louder and louder...

VIVIEN: What can we do?

GEORGE: Fire! Fire! Water. We need water. In the yard Vivien. Run!

252

George and Vivien run back and forward on their lines, Edie stands still in the background clutching her tallybox.

EDIE: Runnin' in the dark. I was running but I felt I was walkin' through mud.

GEORGE: Everyone out! Everyone in the yard! Every hut clear! Leave your things!

EDIE: I didn't think I'd get to my boy on time.

VIVIEN: We've got water! We've got water ready! Buckets and a hose!

GEORGE: All the kids out. Out! Count the kids. Count your kids! It's the straw. It's like a tinderbox.

EDIE: That Jerry was so loud above us.

VIVIEN: Is everyone out? Here comes the water!

GEORGE: Two, two huts have gone up. The others are all right.

EDIE: We fell down and Georgie screamed and screamed.

VIVIEN: They're all out. They're all out. All O.K. We've counted.

GEORGE: We've got it. We've got it now. It's under control.

Edie comes into the present.

EDIE: I felt as if the ground were shakin' all over again. As if the bombs were fallin'.

GEORGE: It was the straw. The straw was alight. Too near the campfire.

EDIE: As if the plane was burnin'.

VIVIEN: The campfire was nowhere near the huts. Nowhere near them.

Pause.

EDIE: No more burning. The fire is over. Over.

GEORGE: You all right?

VIVIEN: Yeah. Yeah I'm fine. You?

GEORGE: He must have known there were people in there.

VIVIEN: You goin' to call the police?

GEORGE: Think I'll 'ave to.

VIVIEN: We can't be sure it was him.

GEORGE: You tryin' to protect him Vivien?

VIVIEN: No. I just don't want no more trouble. I'll go. If I wasn't here none of this would have 'appened.

GEORGE: He's a bully. You don't stand up to a bully by runnin' away. Believe me. I know.

254

Vivien looks at George then walks off. Edie puts down the tallybox and comes forward.

Edie's memory 8: Leave.

EDIE: I was out looking for Georgie. Georgie! Supper! Time to come in! And I saw someone in the distance, too big for Georgie, too weary in the body for a child. He was looking round the fields as if he was trying to find his way. Then I ran, as fast as I could. I had to catch him, make sure he didn't disappear. Alf? Alf is that you? We wasn't expectin' you. What are you doing home?

ALF: Some welcome that is.

EDIE: No it's wonderful. It's a wonderful surprise. Don't you look so smart, so handsome in your uniform? What have you done to your face? You 'aven't been in a fight?

ALF: No. It's nothing. Bumpy landing last week.

EDIE: What do you mean, bumpy landin'?

ALF: We had a little trouble but we got down safely.

EDIE: Thank God. I don't like to think of it.

ALF: Better you don't.

EDIE: You're thinner.

ALF: Well they keep us fit don't they? And the rest of the country's on rations you know.

EDIE: So are we.

ALF: Yeah with your fresh eggs and milk and chickens.

EDIE: And the odd pig.

ALF: Now that is not allowed.

EDIE: Well don't tell anyone. Come on let's go and get Georgie. He'll be so pleased to see you. Georgie! Georgie! Look who's here.

George enters and stares at Alf.

EDIE: It's all right George. It's your dad.

ALF: Yeah it's me Georgie.

GEORGE: You're a soldier.

ALF: A gunner I am George. Air-gunner up in a big plane. They call me the Tail-end Charlie. I shoot all the Jerries; k-pow k-pow, k-pow!

EDIE: Alf stop that. It'll upset him.

GEORGE: I want to go up in a plane.

EDIE: No.

ALF: Maybe when you're bigger.

EDIE: Oh no you don't. One is enough.

GEORGE: But I want to be the pilot.

ALF: Is that right, you toe-rag? Come on then, you be the pilot, I'll be the gunner.

Alf and George play.

GEORGE: Dad what's it like being up in the sky?

ALF: Fantastic. You can see the coast of England like a line and all the fields like little squares below.

EDIE: How long Alf? Are you back for long?

ALF: Tonight.

EDIE: Tonight? One night? Is that all? I thought you 'ad leave.

ALF: I'm on a twenty-four hour pass Edie. I was lucky to get it. Some blokes live too far away. They won't see their wives before they go.

EDIE: Go where?

ALF: They don't tell us love.

EDIE: You mean you won't tell me.

ALF: All I know is it's big this time. That's a good thing. It means it'll be over soon.

EDIE: Do you think so? Do you think this'll be the end and you'll be able to come home?

ALF: Maybe.

EDIE: It's got to end sometime Alf, hasn't it?

ALF: If we win. But we will. We will win.

EDIE: And you'll come back. You'll stop flyin' and you'll come back. *Alf says nothing.* Georgie go in. Supper's ready. Wash your hands.

ALF: Don't send him away.

EDIE: You've come to say goodbye. That's why you're here. Just in case.

ALF: I've got twenty-four hours.

EDIE: It's not enough. *Pause.* We tried to be ordinary for George's sake. We played cards with him, ate our supper, tucked Georgie up. Then we walked out into the hop garden, where it all began and we remembered, we tried to remember everything.

ALF: Saw ya! Saw ya miles off.

EDIE: 1,2,3, the devil's after me, 4,5,6, he's always throwin' sticks, 7,8,9, he misses every time, hallelujah, hallelujah, amen!

ALF: You looked different. All grown up. The smell of the hops in the rain in the kiln. My arms around you

EDIE: Your kiss, soft and sweet on my lips. Me and you and the hopping always.

ALF: A good harvest. All our lives ahead of us. Honest work in God's earth, a sup of cider and a man who loves you.

EDIE: But there's always a tally. There's always a price to be paid. And when the sun rose over the hop fields, my Alf left our bed and I had to let him go, I thought of God the tallyman and feared him.

Edie begins to work.

Singing:

When he cometh, when he cometh to take up his jewels
All his jewels precious jewels his loved and his own
Like the stars of the morning his bright crown adorning
They shall shine in their beauty bright gems for his crown

Woman comes on with telegram.

WOMAN: Edie, Edie, stop a minute.

EDIE: 'Ang on. I'll just finish this bine and get weighed.

WOMAN: No Edie. *Gives telegram.* I'm so sorry.

EDIE: He made it back. Like he always did. Lucky lad they called him. Seventy-four raids in a row. Quite a record they said. The young WAAF who picked 'em up was a new driver. She didn't know her way in the blackout. The truck was packed with air crew all in a hurry to get back to the billet. She lost control, skidded down a bank went over and over. Most of them got out but not Alf, not this time. Sometimes I see a shadow which looks like him, down by the bottom field. Sometimes I think he waves to say, don't worry I'm just down 'ere if you need me. And I walk down, but it's just a shadow and Alf wouldn't want me to be starin' at shadows. He'd want me to get back up the field and ready for the mornin'. Out in the hop garden pickin' in the harvest.

Singing:

It's time to go a 'oppin
It is that time of year
We laugh as we get ready
We'll soon be out of 'ere
Wiv an eh ih oh
Wiv an eh ih oh
Wiv an eh ih ehih oh

Scene Nine.

The hop garden. The transistor radio is playing. George is up on stilts showing off, moving to the music. Vivien is laughing.

VIVIEN: Come on. My turn!

GEORGE: It's not as easy as it looks.

VIVIEN: I want a go!

GEORGE: All right. All right. *He jumps down and holds them out to her. She tries to get up. He holds her on while she tries to walk along.* Careful!

VIVIEN: Keep a hold of me!

GEORGE: I've got you!

VIVIEN: All right. I think I'm OK. You can let go.

GEORGE: You'll fall.

VIVIEN: No I won't. I won't move. I'll just balance. *George lets go and Vivien stands still without falling.* See! I can do it, I can do it!

GEORGE: That's good. That's very good. How does it feel?

VIVIEN: Fantastic. You can see for miles from up 'ere George. Miles and miles. You didn't tell me that.

GEORGE: Well, some things you should try for yourself.

VIVIEN: I'm goin' to try to walk. Just a bit.

GEORGE: Watch it! *Vivien takes a step then wobbles.* It's all right. I'll catch you.

VIVIEN: I'm all right! I'm gettin' down now. Help me. *George helps her down from the stilts then holds her for a minute. She smiles.* It's not that difficult.

GEORGE: Is that right?

VIVIEN: Reckon I could get the 'ang of it by the end of the week. Better than pickin'.

GEORGE: Sorry. It's not a woman's job.

VIVIEN: What?

GEORGE: Men are stilt walkers. No girls allowed.

VIVIEN: You're kiddin'?

GEORGE: That's the way it is.

VIVIEN: You mean you wouldn't let me up there?

GEORGE: Not to work. You can 'ave a go whenever you like.

VIVIEN: Well all I can say is it's time things changed around 'ere. It's 1957 George. You got to get with it. After all I drove Marshy's flash car when he couldn't. I don't see why I can't walk on some old stilts.

GEORGE: There are lots of hoppin' traditions you don't know about.

VIVIEN: Maybe, but they'll be gone soon. Next year Marshy's machines will take over and I'm beginnin' to think it might be a very good thing.

GEORGE: Machines or no machines, there's one we got to keep if you're goin' to be a proper picker.

VIVIEN: Oh yeah? What's that then?

GEORGE: It's a very old tradition for pretty girls.

VIVIEN: I don't like the sound of this.

GEORGE: You 'ave to be dunked in a hop bin.

VIVIEN: Really? Well I can tell you right now...

GEORGE: You can get out of it of course.

262

VIVIEN: And I suppose you can tell me how.

GEORGE: You have to run up and down each alley. If you don't get caught anywhere in the hop garden, you're safe. But if I catch you, you've had it.

VIVIEN: You? Catch me?

GEORGE: That's what I said.

VIVIEN: I warn you George. I'm a very good runner.

GEORGE: And I warn you Vivien, I may be short. I may 'ave a gammy leg, but I'm fast.

VIVIEN: Bet you can't catch me.

GEORGE: Bet I can. *Vivien throws down the stilts and runs off laughing. George chases her.* I'm catchin' you up!

VIVIEN: No chance. I'll be up and down these alleys before you know it.

GEORGE: Here I come, ready or not. *He catches her and holds her.*

VIVIEN: What happens now?

GEORGE: Well first, you got to give me a kiss.

VIVIEN: I think I might manage that.

They kiss. Edie enters. It should remind us of Edie and Alf earlier. George and Vivien notice Edie. Vivien pushes George towards his mother and goes off.

EDIE: She's not daft that girl.

GEORGE: No she's not.

EDIE: She's stayin' then?

GEORGE: Yeah, she is.

EDIE: Till when?

GEORGE: Till the end of the harvest.

EDIE: And how long are you stayin' Georgie?

GEORGE: The same. I've saved a bit of money.

EDIE: Thought you'd spent it all on that wireless.

GEORGE: Not all of it.

EDIE: I see.

GEORGE: I mean it about flyin' mum.

EDIE: I know. I know you do. *Pause.* You know your dad and I thought we'd be 'ere forever. I tried so 'ard to hold on to him but I couldn't. I had to let him go.

GEORGE: It's not forever mum. I'll come back.

264

EDIE: Course you will. *She strokes his face and looks at him.* Now off you go and get that girl. She's waitin' for you. *He smiles, kisses his mum and runs off. The transistor is left.* There you are Alf. You'd be proud of me now.

Edie looks at the radio picks it up, twiddles with the knobs, smiles and goes off with it.

Scene Ten.

The hop kiln. 1957. George is relaxing and listening to his new transistor radio. Enter Vivien. For a minute he doesn't spot her and she stands still watching him and waiting for him to notice. He does so and turns the music down.

GEORGE: How long have you been there?

VIVIEN: Not long. Don't turn your music down. I like it.

GEORGE: Come in.

VIVIEN: Your mum give you back your transistor then?

GEORGE: Yeah, eventually. I think she's taken a shine to it. She found some music that wasn't rock 'n roll.

VIVIEN: This place is fantastic.

GEORGE: You never been in a hop kiln? You did me a favour. I sleep like a log in 'ere. In among the drowsy 'ops.

VIVIEN: What?

GEORGE: They make you sleepy. Pickers can never get up in the mornin'.

VIVIEN: I like that. Drowsy 'ops.

GEORGE: Give you dreams see.

VIVIEN: So this is where you get it from. .

GEORGE: Look up. That's where they tip 'em down, and they float like snowflakes. You're looking at pubs-full of beer. When I was small I used to sneak in 'ere. I liked to see the yellow sulphur sticks in go in. Like fireworks they were, flarin' and burnin'.

VIVIEN: What were they for?

GEORGE: Preservative. Makes your spuds taste funny though.

VIVIEN: What do you mean spuds?

GEORGE: At the end of an hoppin', we come in 'ere and bake potatoes in the fire. But they're hot. You have to watch cos if you're greedy you end up with a burnt lip. Be a shame to burn yours. *He touches Vivien's face.*

The Alf and Edie from 1932 run in with their cider and potatoes. George and Vivien do not see them.

EDIE: You're a rascal you are Alf. We're not supposed to be in here.

ALF: Who says?

EDIE: My mum for one.

ALF: Your mum don't want me with you at all. Anywhere.

EDIE: I know.

ALF: A nice chap like me. She don't know how lucky you are.

EDIE: Cheeky so and so.

ALF: It's true. I'm a good catch I am.

EDIE: Are you now? Still, I can't see them changin'.

ALF: I'll win her round. You'll see.

EDIE: I hope so Alf.

ALF: Your mum would like a tot of cider herself. If she got the chance.

EDIE: Don't be daft. My mum don't drink.

ALF: She tell you that? Bet she has a sly one during them hymns.

EDIE: She don't!

ALF: Those long sermons then. You'd have to have somethin'. Smell those hops. *Edie takes a breath in.* What is it?

EDIE: It's the autumn. I can smell it. Smelt it this mornin' when I got up.

ALF: Cheer up. I got potatoes to roast.

EDIE: Have you?

ALF: Yeah it's a feast for you Edie. Cider and hot potatoes cooked in the kiln. What more can a girl want?

EDIE: Nothin'. Cider and potatoes will do me. *Edie and Alf remain looking at each other. Vivien gets up and twirls round the kiln.*

VIVIEN: You really goin' to fly me to Monte Carlo?

GEORGE: I thought I might. You'll 'ave to wait a bit though.

VIVIEN: You're all the same you men. We always 'ave to wait.

GEORGE: Not long. I promise. *Vivien twirls back and looks down at George, smiling.*

ALF: Edie?

EDIE: Yeah.

ALF: How would it be if this time you stayed?

EDIE: I can't stay. I got a job back in London.

ALF: You could have a job here.

EDIE: Not much call for a factory girl on a farm.

ALF: No I mean you could do a different job.

EDIE: And what would that be?

ALF: Well I don't know, but if you were my wife I'd work your fingers to the bone.

EDIE: Your wife?

ALF: I don't want you to go back Edie, not this time, not again. Stay here and marry me. Well will you?

EDIE: What do you think? *Alf pulls Edie to her feet.*

ALF: Edie!

EDIE: Coming. *She looks over to George and Vivien and goes off with Alf. Vivien takes George's hand and pulls him to his feet.*

VIVIEN: Come on George. Let's make the most of this radio. We can dance.

GEORGE: Dance? In 'ere?

VIVIEN: Anywhere. Dancin' or flyin', we're goin' places.

Vivien turns up the radio and they dance. Fade to blackout

Forest Forge Theatre Company is supported by

The company's technical equipment is sponsored by